Playing Life from Center Court

*The Ultimate Guide
to Emotional Fitness:
Living without Anger and Fear*

By Emotional Fitness Coach
Arynne A. Simon, Ph.D.

Foreword by Steve Wozniak

SelectBooks, Inc.
New York

Playing Life from Center Court
Copyright 2004 © by Arynne A. Simon

This edition published by SelectBooks, Inc. For information address
SelectBooks, Inc., New York, New York.

First Edition

ISBN 1-59079-060-X

Library of Congress Cataloging-in-Publication Data

Simon, Arynne A., 1936–

Playing life from center court: the ultimate way to emotional fitness:
living without anger and fear / by emotional fitness coach, Arynne
A. Simon; foreword by Steve Wozniak.– 1st ed.

p. cm.

ISBN 1-59079-060-X (hardbound : alk. paper)

1. Emotional intelligence. I. Title.

BF576.S585 2004
152.4–dc22
2004003615

Manufactured in the United States of America

10 9 8 7 6 5 4 3 2 1

*For Minerva Lobel Abeles and
the Honorable Peter Aaron Abeles,
my adored and admired parents.*

Contents

Foreword

By Steve Wozniak

Henry Kissinger was once heard to comment on how life had changed due to his fame and popularity; he said, "Now when I bore people at parties, they think it's their fault." I confess to enjoying this experience now as well, although I have learned to listen better than ever as a result of working with youngsters.

The ability to listen may be even harder than the ability to make someone laugh. I have tried to learn the meaning of quality listening, and I continue to try very hard to learn from what others say. But laughter still gives me the greatest high, and I believe that laughter is an integral part of learning. If I listen, think, and am able to laugh, I know I will have learned.

But the learning process begins by paying attention to smart people. Since most people don't listen to each other, many end up chasing after more and more how-to-books and seminars and psychologists. And they are not all as good for you as the perpetrators of those books and courses would have you believe. These behavior experts abound because people have stopped listening to each other. Many people have forgotten how to laugh, but I sometimes think that most of us have never learned how to listen. Some of us who may know how to listen may have forgotten how to really hear what others say, or may brush aside ideas that don't immediately appeal to them.

Arynne Simon is an exception—a teacher and consultant with a Ph.D.—and her communication skills reinvigorate the sport of listening. People who have learned from Arynne have been urging for years that she share her unique ideas on how to be more effective in dealing with others. She teaches the skills upon which a satisfying life is built and preserved. I like best that she dislikes the idea of networking and hopes that people will form relationships that give to others as well as getting what they need.

Some people can inspire you to aim for the stars and to dream of achievements that will bring you fulfillment, satisfaction, and delight. Some people can feed your soul with spiritual food and laughter. Steve Wozniak says: Find those people and listen to them. Listen to them and hear what they have to say. As Arynne Simon says, you have the right to retain the final decision and do it your own way. Listening takes courage. As Winston Churchill said, "It takes courage to speak your mind, but it takes even more courage to listen to what others have to say." Reading books like this one is a form of attentive listening.

Steve Wozniak

Acknowledgements

I had long been resistant about transforming my spoken words—currently heard in group seminars, on cassettes and CD, and in one-to-one coaching sessions—into a book for people who prefer to learn by reading rather than by listening. My extraordinary husband, known to his readers and publishers as bestselling author William L. Simon, and my dear friend and associate Joanne (Mrs. Hal) Carroll nagged, coerced, and even bribed me to "just do it." Joanne decided to transpose my spoken words into computer text to entice me forward. To Joanne I will always be most warmly grateful, for this book has launched me enthusiastically into a new phase of my career as writer—something my husband has been encouraging for so many years. And, YES, two more books are already in the works.

This book would not have become a reality without my darling husband, who reviewed and put his professional polish on every word, sentence, and idea. Will, as I call him, even generously shared with me his illustrious agent Bill Gladstone, and together they persisted until Kenzi Sugihara, CEO of Select Books, said "yes" to publishing the work of a first-time writer, me. Kenzi is a jewel of a man to work with—nirvana for a writer. His assigned editor, Todd Barmann, deserves my thanks for his detailed input and practical suggestions to make this book even easier for everyone to enjoy and use.

Special thanks to my many friends, going all the way back to a kind lady named Margaret Hough, from Del Mar, California, who was the first to say to me, "Arynne, I want to help you write a book so that your ideas can change the lives of many, many more people." Over the past twenty years or so I have lost touch with Margaret, but her words and enthusiasm for my teachings have kept me motivated and focused.

For more than twenty-five years, I've been teaching these principles and others to so many people. It may seem an exaggeration, but mega-thousands have been "Simonized by Arynne;" and many have become close, treasured friends. I owe so many people more than mere acknowledgement; each one deserves my individual thanks and a special hug for encouraging me and for giving me the ultimate high of being able to impact their lives as a friend, mentor, and teacher.

Tender thanks goes to my son, Sheldon Bermont; my daughter, Victoria Simon, Ph.D.; to Josie Rodriguez, and to Jessica Dudgeon. Also, I include appreciation for special friends Walt and Linda Brown, Linda Lawrence, Mike and Chris Steep , Karen Settle, and Marjorie Linglet, all part of a very close inner circle of people who bring me both joy and stability, and often act as a sounding board for my ideas.

This first book acknowledges the impact made on me by my honorable mother, Minerva L. Abeles, whose influence, like my favorite color yellow, has cast a sunny light over my life.

Introduction

My Mother Was a Typewriter.

The early 1900's was a titillating time for young women who delighted in their new financial emancipation. Those were the days of the Gibson girl and young stenographers shopping at B. Altman and Company for silk stockings with embroidered patterns called "clocks." Back then, the new piece of office equipment was known as a *typing machine,* and the young people operating them were known as *typewriters.*

My mother was proud of being a typewriter, in company with the other savvy young office professionals Minerva was trained in stenography as well as typing, and was fluent in four languages. Despite a pampered private life, she was most proud of a degree from Hunter College High School. In the high spirit of New York in the Wharton era, she could communicate in a man's world because of her keen sense of humor. She could recount amusing anecdotes with accurate dialects or in any of several languages. My mother cherished laughter even over kindness. And all this was the basis of the values she would set for me; "love, laugh, and learn" was the admonition absorbed by all her children.

The wildness of New York in the early nineteen-hundreds satisfied my mother's longing for freedom and adventure. Her dimples and white lawn dresses were a modest packaging for the proud and feisty independence she would carry through her long and vigorous life, and her beauty and enviable health were valuable assets in those days of tight corsets and offices reachable only by long flights of splintered wooden stairs. She lived without fear in a rapidly changing world that looked promising despite the squalor and brutality present in the inner city. She was born before electric lights were commonplace and lived to see Neil Armstrong walk on the moon.

When any of us (there were five) went to her with a question, we could always count on getting a surprising response that in today's corporate lingo would be described as "out of the box thinking." An answer from our dad was rigidly Republican, expectedly traditional, yet always human. Peter, as a New York State Senator, was known as "the people's friend" because it was his legislation that prevented landlords from evicting renters onto the street for non-payment. Minerva often disagreed with him and had the courage to face him on a verbal battlefield of ideas. When "togetherness" meant that a married couple always agreed, my father made clear that the differing opinions of our parents were only two of many possible choices.

You will find that this book carries my parents' tradition of inviting into every discussion many differing perspectives. My dad loved the United States, and held elected office to protect the laws and traditions of this country. However he once said to me, and I was sure it was a metaphor my mother had dreamed up, that Howard Johnson was the keeper of this nation's Democracy. After all, Dad said, no other country ever thought of offering 28 flavors of ice cream.

My mother participated in politics, campaigning alongside Eleanor Roosevelt and managing the campaign of one of New York's most famous mayors, Fiorello LaGuardia. She was a dynamic addition to the lives of many people. Only when well satisfied that her family was cared for did she venture out into the community to "do her own thing." Those were the days when men, to whom the kitchen was off-limits, gave permission for women to volunteer in the community. She trained me to teach people how they might combine work with a fine and supportive home life. She encouraged me to set an example of loving, caring, and independence.

But as Minerva grew older, there was one thing that bothered her enough to make her complain with a negative clarity I had never heard before. This lady who had fought for women's right to vote began to criticize the behavior of women whose brashness she was observing on television. She would eventually say that women did not belong in politics or business. My mother struggled to express what she thought had gone wrong with working women, but although something was bothering her, she could not accurately analyze the problem.

I now realize that 1886, the year she was born, was also the year that Freud published his first work. The people of her generation came late to a psychological vocabulary. They knew words for 'love,' 'anger,' and 'hate,' but they described nervousness as 'butterflies' or 'vapors'. There were no such phrases as "sibling rivalry," nor an understanding of aggressive behavior, and the principles of what we now call "assertive behavior"—a cornerstone of this book—were still a long way in the future.

The emotional language that Freud developed is great when two psychologists talk to each other. But for most people, a statement like 'I'm jealous' masks the real feelings involved. My mother, who understood her own feelings better, said things like, "I'm frightened when you come home late," and "I'm angry that you don't care enough about me to get home on time. Sorry, dear, your dinner is ruined." I learned that a description of a basic feeling is a far better form of communication.

My mother taught me to communicate in specifics. She described to me how the modern working women and men were behaving and then left it to me to figure out. And, as you will see, I did.

I came to realize what my mother meant after I had been in the business world for so many years. Indeed, I saw women and men being dramatically emotional: over-reacting when they were criticized, overly verbal when disagreeing, describing current events in terms of extreme danger. The new breed of workers were treating their work environments like home, making friends with managers and treating co-workers as family. In the process, they were squandering huge amounts of their emotional energies in the workplace while skewing the proper flow and control of their emotions in their personal lives. Not a good set up for a life without stress.

As you'll learn in this book, emotions are muscles; and when they are firm and strong, they are ready to be used when you want to use them. At the age of three, my daughter Victoria had trouble remembering which was the hot water faucet. She'd get confused and turn on the hot water when she wanted cold. She soon learned which faucet would get her a cool glass of water and she learned how to mix hot and cold to a useful temperature for washing. I have become aware that emotional faucets are harder to sort out.

The emotionally fit person feels all emotions, but knows which faucet to turn on, and when. Unless you're emotionally fit, you can't manage the mix. Emotional Fitness will keep you in charge of your emotional muscles. Believe me, they're easier to strengthen than stomach muscles.

I don't want this book to be just another inspirational/motivational sermon. I have designed it as a precise program. It is not a high-powered emotional fix, like some of the programs being taught these days. But at the back of this book you will find the address for sending me your e-mail of thanks when you feel like telling me, as so many others have, that your life is much better now that you've been "Simonized."

You are about to see how I have transformed psychological information into a set of easy behaviors, just as the complicated science of body chemistry becomes a sensible diet. The crash diet is as harmful and unrealistic as high-powered motivational courses that promise more than they can deliver. I promise a lot and deliver even more. You will see.

I'm delighted I have been able to identify and find a solution to a problem my mother couldn't even describe. For over twenty-five years I have been giving people the coaching they need to improve their emotional muscle tone and to succeed at home and at work. If you are a parent, this book will help get you through your children's growing-up years. If you are a significant other, you will listen to your partner's trouble with a boss or a needy friend and still be able to sleep through the night. To stay in "center court," your muscle tone needs to be reliably fit. Emotional fitness can rid you of anger and fear. And that's not science fiction, it is a reality you can achieve.

This book gives you the opportunity to be in charge of your life, to be emotionally independent. If there are people in your life who are causing unpleasant situations, after just a few chapters you'll be able to approach them and resolve some of these seemingly insurmountable problems. I'll teach you to accept reality, but give you the skills to modify it when necessary. The best way to learn is to do so at your own pace, in a civilized manner, with your self-respect kept intact.

Most people carry emotional "flab" and do whatever they can to avoid unpleasant realities. But it doesn't work. Ignoring life's realities will backfire. People suffer for a long time from anger and fear because they don't have the skills to face up to their anxieties and solve them. You can get by without Emotional Fitness, but with it you will be tuned into a better quality life. Don't be satisfied with just getting by. The guidance in this book can get you off the psychological merry-go-round, out of the emotional yo-yo syndrome. It can get you into fit condition and then keep you there.

1

Playing in Center Court

I Discover Racquetball

When I first arrived in California, I headed straight for the tennis courts to begin a program that required sets of chic tennis outfits. But within months, despite the promises made by my California friends, the rains came pouring down and the mirror announced that my golden tan was fading during that too-long spell of clouds and showers.

From my emotional memory bank I pulled out a bit of my mother's wisdom—unfashionably original advice when I first heard it, but words that have become standard in parenting vocabularies thanks to the Julie Andrews line in *The Sound of Music:* "When God closes a door, he opens a window." If the tennis courts were turning into nesting spots for ducks, it would be up to me to find a substitute. In the days when it was rare to see a walker or runner along the side of the road, I was way ahead of the physical fitness craze and into daily aerobics. But then a window blew open and I discovered the game of racquetball.

I immediately connected to the wildly aggressive sound of the bouncing ball. In those early days of this new sport we used a ball of intense blue, and I responded to the bouncing ball the same way I did as a kid in the movie theatres of New York to the bouncing ball on the screen during the sing-alongs—with wild enthusiasm. Chasing after it provided the sweat and the heartbeat and the competitive challenge. What a great way to start any day.

My three partners and I (yes, we started out playing doubles) pursued that wild little ball, and because I had never been a handball or squash player, it tricked me every time. I found myself chasing after it with a vengeance—running into walls and slamming into my partners. When the ball found a corner, I tried to flick it up with that special motion I saw some experienced players using. But the paddle would end up hitting my face and the blue demon would dribble onto my feet. On a daily basis I paddled myself or my partner, with either the racquet or the ball.

True, I was achieving my exercise goals—but a new challenge was being created. I was determined to master this game. I would ignore the black and blue marks and the swollen eyes. I was hooked, obsessed, or motivated—depending on whom I talked to. Many people suggested going back to the tennis courts, but I ignored the sun and found a racquetball coach.

Ron was a tennis player who had latched onto the growing enthusiasm for this new game and promised to teach me winning skills. He diplomatically mentioned the fact that I often looked like a battered wife, brought protective goggles to our first lesson, and insisted that I stop running after the ball—an instruction that I didn't buy, as it seem to make no sense at all at the time.

Finally I began to think ahead. I stopped running into the walls and developed some timing, waiting for the ball to come to me. When the ball hit a wall, I learned to anticipate where it would bounce and get into position to take a proper swing. In learning the new rhythm this game required, I learned what hockey player Wayne Gretsky describes as "getting to know where the puck [or ball] is *going* to be." I began to understand how the ball bounces.

Physical fitness was an expected benefit of my two-hour playing ritual. But those of you who exercise regularly, whether you bike, walk, run, or lift weights, know that soon the brain finds its own place to go—a space beyond the action, where new ideas and feelings are discovered. This special place beyond the sweat and strain can actually be explored while the physical exercise is being done. Over time, emotional calm becomes an intrinsic benefit of physical fitness, as the brain is freed to explore in new and stress-free ways.

When Ron introduced me to the concept of Center Court, I began to rack up points even against many of the best competitive players around the facility. Soon I realized that whoever controlled Center Court generally won the points. It was not about the ball or who could run faster, it was about owning Center Court. And I began to find ways to force my opponents into corners; I found ways to get them chasing back and forth after the ball. It even helped my tennis game because I was learning that in any aggressive game, that's what must be done to win—put your opponents into the tough corners. Just force them out of Center Court.

Because I was playing from Center Court, my bruises began to heal. Soon Center Court became a symbol for me, a symbol of winning.

My students were soon relieved to see the bruises fade; a few admitting to having wondered about my black-and-blue marks. Thinking back to that rainy season, I now realize what a profitable experience was provided for me. Out of the bruises and a new game came a concept of a racquetball court as a perfect way to teach the fundamental concept of EMOTIONAL FITNESS.

Racquetball Is Not an Assertive Game

Racquetball is an aggressive, potentially bruising game. It is possible that Emotional Fitness is going to teach you be an aggressive winner; but that is not my goal, and I hope it's not yours.

Sports like racquetball are meant to be *aggressive*—where one person is clearly the winner and the other loses. So I use it only to illustrate an important point: if you operate in life out of the corners that I have named Fear and Anger, you don't stand much of a chance to enjoy the "game of life." In racquetball or tennis, the goal is to own Center Court and drive others out of a winning position. In life, your goal would best be different. In the game of life, it would be better to encourage others into Center Court with you.

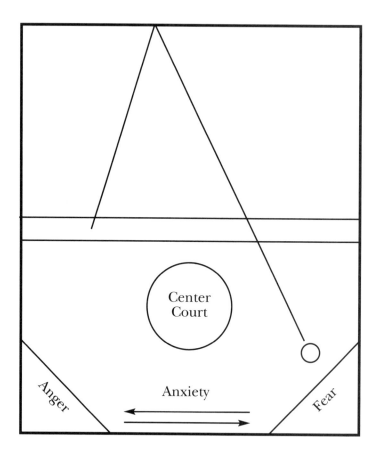

If I were writing a physical fitness book, it would be easy to include photographs and illustrations of various activities with their positions and movements clearly demonstrated. It's tougher when discussing concepts and feelings—there's no visualization that can help. But this simplified diagram of a racquetball court will help you to visualize and remember your feelings. I've had great success using this diagram, for it takes a pragmatic approach that leads to rapid results. However, a disclaimer is in order: because no metaphor, symbol, or analogy is a perfect fit—I ask you to be flexible and use the illustrations to help you understand the basic concepts of Emotional Fitness.

The Racquetball Analogy & the Corners of 'Anger' and 'Fear'

Most of you have seen a racquetball court, and will notice on the diagram that there's a large circle in the center which you'd never find painted on a real court. This general area is what I refer to as CENTER COURT.

When playing racquetball from Center Court, you can force your opponent to dash madly back and forth from one back corner to the other by hitting the ball into the corners. If you manage to continuously get the ball far back into those comers, you will gain control of the point by exhausting a typical competitor. As I've explained, beginners find those corners frustrating, and they can be painful if you run for a ball in the comer and swing wildly in an attempt to return it. If you're playing to win you'll be out of control, and even your opponent would best get out of your way. That's how beginners play—running after the ball, and into each other.

As I played the game, my background and training nudged my mind into labeling those corners Anger and Fear—the two most painful of the basic human emotions. In life, isn't it true that when you get angry it not only hurts you, but it also hurts anyone who gets near you?

Arynne **SIMON SAYS**

Anger + Fear = Anxiety

Please study the diagram again. I'd like you to notice the area along the back wall between Anger and Fear—the arrows labeled Anxiety. On the racquetball court, as a new player you're probably dashing back and forth between the two corners and working up a good sweat. But believe me, you're about to lose the point. Once your opponent has you chasing the ball between the two corners, you'll soon wear out. In a state of confusion you'll not get a chance to get a really good swing at the ball.

Let's translate that concept into Emotional Fitness. Running between Anger and Fear is a good description of anxiety. Anxiety is the combination of Anger and Fear, and you know that when Anger and Fear exist at the same time, you feel worn out. When anxiety sets in, the chance for making a smart decision is minimal.

The primary goal of Emotional Fitness is to get you out of life's corners of Anger and Fear and into playing life from Center Court—where problems can be solved and contentment exists. But unlike a competitive game, the Center Court of life would best be a place for you to share with everyone who wants to live a win-win life with you. Unfortunately, not everyone wants to play life from Center Court; and there are those who will want to own Center Court by driving you out. Hopefully, after reading this book you will know how to stay in Center Court and not be driven back into anxiety. But at least I'd like you to find ways to encourage others into Center Court with you.

Inherent throughout this discussion is the concept of 'assertiveness' versus 'aggressiveness,' and you will learn more about the differences between 'assertive' and 'aggressive' as you complete this book. It's my personal view that aggressive competition needs to be thought of in an entirely new light, from the schoolyard straight up through the halls of business. This regimen, as any true learning experience, is for people who can digest new concepts and move forward with them. To assist you in doing so, and in becoming emotionally fit and emotionally independent for life, I use some familiar psychological terms with my own definitions. The definitions used in this book are not the ones you would learn in a psychology classroom, but they work for turning passive or aggressive people into assertive, emotionally fit people.

So, if your kids are driving you nuts with their "sibling rivalry," what's really going on? If your manager is jealous of your friendship with the boss, how can you get to a place where that doesn't bother you? If your neighbor is "passive/aggressive," what does that mean and how can you handle sharing a fence with him/her?

Anger and Fear Exist in Many Combinations

Many years ago for a Christmas party, I made some thirty varieties of bread from recipes gathered from Ireland to the Ivory Coast, and served them with local cheeses and wines. In the process I learned much about the countries of origin and their traditions, as well as this interesting item: that bread is always a mixture of grain and liquid. Essentially, flour and liquid combine to form the generic product called 'bread'. There are many varieties of bread, each with its own idiosyncratic differences. But the base is always a mixture of flour and liquid.

When I studied painting, I learned that all skin tone is made up of two colors: red and yellow. While teaching art at the Corcoran Museum of Art in Washington, D.C., I explained to a group of youngsters that skins are all different combinations of the colors red and yellow. The very pale skin color that is called white is made up of very pale red (pink) and very pale yellow (cream). Very dark skin is made up of deeper shades of red and yellow. But all skin tone is basically made up of only two colors. Their faces beamed with delight at this information, and I hoped they would see themselves and the world in a very different light with this new information.

When one realizes how many variations of skin tone are possible just from different combinations of reds and yellows, and how many different varieties of bread are possible from flour and liquid, you'll also understand the variations of negative feelings that are possible combinations of Anger and Fear. Consider the word 'anxiety' as a generic description of the combination of Anger and Fear, with psychological buzzwords like 'jealousy' and 'guilt' merely representing different combinations of Anger and Fear. So what is jealousy? It often expresses some intense, hidden Fear: "My husband kept glancing over at that girl with the low-cut blouse. What will happen to me if my husband leaves me? What will my friends say? Will my family think I did something wrong? Maybe I'll be left alone and no one will ever want me." Jealousy also contains Anger: "He shouldn't treat me that way, and I shouldn't be a doormat and put up with it!" You will learn in the pages on Anger how jealousy contains Anger. And in a special mix of Fear and Anger, jealousy becomes a specific form of anxiety.

Simply put, Anger and Fear in different combinations cause all negative emotions: guilt, jealousy, rivalry, revenge, passive aggressiveness, etc Anxiety is like bread. Flat breads, risen breads, breads with shiny crusts, breads that pop up—all are made from two basic ingredients.

Emotional Fitness allows for a much easier, and much more direct, analysis of your feelings by thinking only in terms of Anger and Fear. 'Sibling rivalry' becomes clear when you know that a child is afraid of losing a place of prime importance in a parent's life, and is angry that a new baby might usurp his/her attention or position. A manager's 'jealousy' might be better explained as an anxiety that mixes Fear of losing image with Anger that his/her work is not being sufficiently acknowledged by the company. Be courageous. Most people, men especially, will deny all existence of Fear. Use your own powers of observation and intuition to figure out what the Fear and Anger are.

I have found that it's wasteful to try to find a solution to sibling rivalry or jealousy; but that there are, indeed, ways to quiet and calm the components of anxiety—the Fear and Anger that become lethal when mixed. So when you feel that wild, out-of-control, out-of-center-court feeling, you'll now find that it's far more effective to call it anxiety and begin to search into the causes of Fear and Anger. And in the upcoming pages you'll learn how to do just that.

Winning and Emotional Fitness

After I developed my understanding of racquetball, I could actually win twenty-one serves in a row. My husband and his friends were very good tennis players, much better than I ever was, but they couldn't play racquetball as well as I could. They didn't have a chance against me to get out into Center Court and get a real flick at the ball. It was fun for a while to be able to outplay everybody. But then I began to find it rather dull—my opponent was always back in the corners, giving me no real competition, and I even lost my chance for exercise. I was winning without sweating but no longer enjoying the game.

When you play a game for points, it's true you must be an aggressive player—but the game of life is not played on a racquetball court. The game of life for an aggressive player is a lonely, empty place. Since I'm using examples from games and sports to clarify and teach Emotional Fitness, I'd like to be sure we're on the same page with a definition of "winning." In a game, it's obvious that the goal is to attain a certain number of points before your opponent does. You can say you've had a fun game, but if you intend to be champion for the day, points are the way to clearly win. The outcome is obviously measured in numbers.

But a win in life is not that clear. Even if *Fortune* magazine continues to measure winning in terms of numbers, life has many other measurements. Most of us accept the standards everyone else seems to follow, so we defer to the person with the most money, the biggest house and the greatest number of articles written about him/her, as the biggest winner in the game of life. Get up close to these people, and many of them neither feel nor behave like winners. I've been close to many supposed winners, and can assure you that the game of life needs better measurements for determining who is a winner and who is not.

There are a lot of gurus these days who say, "Just take care of yourself. Get yourself into a winning position and don't worry about anyone else." Well, there I was in Center Court, all alone. If everyone else is a second-class player, you can look down on them with disdain. Hooray for you; you own the position of being the best player and a sure winner—but an isolated winner. In racquetball you're ready for tournaments, but in life you'd be a big loser and big-time lonely.

True winning has more to do with a whole group of feelings, a sense of being comfortable in the world, of not being lonely, and of being able to live life in forward motion. At the coaching/counseling organization called Talk Works, in Los Angeles, they measure winning in terms of being able to get through life's transitions without more stress than is necessary. Indeed, transitions cause problems for people without emotional muscle tone. A lot of people who play the game of life very aggressively, aiming to win as they would in a sport, turn out to be big losers in terms of their personal relationships and their feelings about themselves.

I'm not saying to hold back your strengths or hide your talents, but it's important to play life as game that encourages others to play successfully alongside you. The game of life is not for points; it's more like a long rally, and it's important to encourage others to get out there with you so you can enhance your own enjoyment of life. The real win is feeling good about yourself and other people, not getting points for yourself while driving your partner's score down.

So can we agree that a win in life is something more complex than the winning of points in a game? Okay—then we can proceed together.

Friends Are Important in Emotional Fitness

There are people who say, as if it were a kind of virtue, "I don't have a lot of friends. I have a few friends, and the others are just acquaintances." It's not a virtue to have just a few friends. For an emotionally fit person, there's no limit to the number of friends you can have. There are all sorts of friendships, and not all need be as close to you as others. But many are friends who can be invited into Center Court with you. The number of friends you have is a valid measure of how emotionally fit you are.

Looking Ahead

As you strive for Center Court, you will come to see the freedom Emotional Fitness affords you. Freedom from Anger and Fear will mean that you can go into any meeting with your mind working clearly. You will be able to handle without stress the problems your children present. You will face everyday dilemmas with calm and confidence, in control and full of energy. You will know the joy of mentally solving transition problems without the noise of your emotions beating wildly in your ears. To play life every day with the skill for handling challenges, not becoming worn out by them, this is the main benefit of Emotional Fitness. It will help you deal with life's many problems just as physical fitness helps you to acquire and maintain a strong and healthy body. And once you learn Emotional Fitness, you won't lose it. It's like getting your balance on a bicycle or learning to swim.

First we need to work on getting rid of Anxiety—that painful waste of effort running between Anger and Fear. Look again at the racquetball diagram to make sure you know that any combination of Anger and Fear is what causes anxiety. As you toss and turn in bed, you're shifting between Anger and Fear. On one side, Anger—"He had no right to do that to me;" and on the other side, Fear—"What will I do if he fires me?" And so the anxiety builds.

The first step in developing the muscles required for Emotional Fitness is to remove one of these negative emotions. Since anxiety is the combination of the two, it won't exist without both of them combined. The easiest negative emotion for most of us to remove is the Anger, and I will show you how to get rid of that in Chapter 2.

EMOTIONAL FITNESS EXERCISES

Here is your first emotional muscle-building exercise. It may seem so simple that it may appear to be without value. Don't be deceived; this exercise is a big step forward towards your goal of Emotional Fitness.

1. Visit a racquetball court if there is one near where you live to see for yourself where Center Court is. See or imagine where the corners of Anger and Fear are, and picture how Anxiety builds up as you run from Anger to Fear. Visualize what you've learned so far in this book. Take the time to do this so the painful feelings of Anger and Fear will become intellectual concepts you can build upon. Then with a pencil on paper, make your own diagram of a racquetball court. Do it on a 3x5 card and post it where you can see it often. It will reinforce your understanding of this important concept.

2. Diagram a problem you now have in terms of the racquetball illustration. Picture yourself on the court. Are you trapped in a corner? List your Fears concerning the problem. List what you're angry about. Separate your Anger from your Fear. Repeat often that any anxiety is a product of running between the two corners. Add to the lists of your Angers and Fears about this one problem that is causing anxiety or stress.

You are now ready to read Chapter 2.

2

Who's in Charge Here?

ARYNNE **SIMON SAYS**

**It's what you learn
after you know it all
that counts.**

Now you're ready to consider some of the barriers that tend to keep you out of Center Court. You will gain more control of your own life by learning to distinguish between *instructions* and *suggestions*, and by becoming aware of the significant difference between power and control.

Slow Down

Let's begin by getting back onto the racquetball court. When a newcomer first starts playing racquetball, the tendency—as I said in Chapter 1—is to run all over the court, to chase madly after the ball. Running into the walls and getting trapped in corners is typical of the beginning player.

If you had a coach when starting out, you would be encouraged to slow down and wait for the ball to come to you. You would learn to anticipate where and how the ball would bounce, and your coach would teach you how to take control of Center Court. You would learn not to react immediately to every movement of the ball. You would learn, as I did, to play the game of racquetball not just physically, but intellectually.

Here, you are learning through Emotional Fitness to handle your emotions in a similar way. You're learning to gain control of your reactions and responses, not by squelching your emotions, but by recognizing them and managing them in a suitable way. By combining your emotions and intellect, you will play life from Center Court, where you can have a sense of being able to judge what's happening around you while seeing life played out at a manageable speed.

One of the first things to do is begin to slow down your thought process and reactions. I have found that separating the implications of familiar words like 'instructions' and 'suggestions' is the best way to begin the process. 'Power' and 'control' are another pair of words that could use careful redefining and a new level of understanding. And in some upcoming pages, you'll be doing the same separation of the words 'want' and 'need'.

Let's start by agreeing that an instruction implies that you must follow it, "or else." When it comes to a suggestion, you're clearly given the choice to decide whether or not you're going to comply. If you're given an instruction, it comes with the implied control of another, while a suggestion gives you the final say. Right?

By 'instructions,' I mean *orders;* by 'suggestions,' *requests or recommendations.* Most people could easily explain the difference between these ordinary words—but when it comes to everyday living, we act as if we don't recognize any difference. As a consequence of this blurring of meaning, most people have a sense of being trapped into doing things they don't want to do—being controlled by people who have no right to have the final say over what they do. As an example, imagine that you walk into a baseball stadium and head for the stairway you regularly use. Along comes an attendant who insists on looking at your tickets and then says you're at the wrong stairway. So he directs you to a different one. You know he's wrong but he's sure he's right, and he's wearing the uniform. Do you do as he says or trust your own judgment?

It's not too soon for you to start getting rid of the feeling that you must always listen to what people tell you to do. If you're regularly on the receiving end of the controlling behavior of another person, you will appreciate this keen awareness of what's been happening in your life. And if you're trying to have final say over the actions of people you have no right to control, this is a fine opportunity to revisit that behavior.

Once you learn the real difference between instructions and suggestions, you'll develop the ability to recognize inappropriate control the moment you hear it and respond appropriately. Life has taught me that whenever there's a struggle between people, it can usually be traced to an unbalanced, inappropriate use of control. By the end of this book, you'll learn to recognize control in its many forms; and more even importantly, you'll learn how to withstand it without becoming a "control freak" yourself.

When Is a Suggestion Not a Suggestion?

When I was a little girl, my mother often *suggested* I wear a sweater. But my mother never gave suggestions, and I knew it deep down inside my heart. And your mother never did, either. I clearly felt my mother's emotional clout even though her instruction to wear a sweater was delivered pleasantly as a suggestion.

Many of us had teachers who wrote on the lower left-hand corner of the blackboard (they were blackboards when I was a little girl) what they called a "suggested" reading list. Any student who hoped to get an 'A' in the course knew perfectly well that it was not a "suggested" list—if you wanted an 'A', you would have to read those books. It would have been more straightforward for the teacher to have written, "Instruction: Read these books if you want to get an 'A' in this course." I'm sure there are suggested lists put up everywhere. It is up to you to determine: which are really "suggested" and which are really instructions.

A boss might say to his admin in a pleasant way, "Would you do me a favor? I suggest you type these letters with wider margins." This very gracious and civilized communication style has implied that there is a choice the secretary can make. This boss knows that a modern manager does not bark his orders, but by suggesting rather than instructing he has given away his final say and has confused the situation. Did he really mean that his administrative assistant now has the final choice? If in fact this boss has made up his mind how he wants the letters done, he's setting the secretary up to fail by making it sound as if the decision is hers. In the way he expressed himself, the seeds of miscommunication are sown; the ground is prepared for Anger and frustration. Clearly, he'd like a way to say what he means without being rude. It would be better if he said simply, "I'd like these letters typed with wider margins."

Don't Be Confused

Many of us have confused the meaning of the word *suggestion* because we've been misusing it, and so have the people around us. But when you take the time to consider it, the difference between instructions and suggestions is obvious—so you think you don't have to pay close attention. As your coach, I urge you to slow down and take another very careful look at these two words. Because once you're able to decide which one is accurate at that moment, you'll no longer feel out of control, driven into the corners of life by others trying to control you. You will be able to refine your listening, enabling you to respond the way you want to, the way that's most appropriate for each particular situation.

Children believe that when they're all grown up, nobody will be able to give them instructions any more, that they're going to be totally in charge of themselves. While you and I know that's not reality, many of us grow up having taken orders from too many people and not being given final say in enough areas of our lives. If that's happened to you, it's possible that you allow people to control areas of your life that really belong to you. Or you might mistakenly balk when someone is in a valid position to give you instructions—such as your boss or a traffic cop.

What you're learning now is dependent on your understanding of which areas of control—final say—are yours, and which belong to others. Once you're clear on that, you will learn to respond appropriately to the way things are. You may come to the conclusion that you don't like some of the things that make up your reality, but perhaps with new skills you'll be able to change them.

Put on Your Third Ear

Many times the literal translation of a foreign phrase is not at all what it really means. In such cases, language experts learn to interpret and identify the real meaning behind the words. That's what you can learn to do by putting on your "third ear"—an adult listening ear. As an adult, when you receive verbal messages from others, it's up to you to sort them out. You can decide whether what you're hearing is actually what the words are saying or if, in fact, the words imply something else—like my mother *suggesting* the sweater when she was really telling me to wear it.

It's no secret that people often don't say what they mean. It's up to you to interpret, to hear what is actually being said. The ears you were born with are emotional ears—connected to your feelings. These baby ears hear everything emotionally, and only as it relates to your own sense of what is safe and good for you. As an adult, you must train yourself to hear intellectually if you hope to sort out the speaker's true intent.

Your trained "third ear" will help you to hear more correctly what others are actually intending instead of just what they say. Only then can your newly learned emotional fitness skills assist you to respond accurately. If you're still hearing suggestions from everyone as instructions, then you are wearing an outgrown set of ears.

Find Out When You're Not In Control

So how do you begin taking control away from people who are giving you instructions when they only have the right to be giving you suggestions? The first step is deciding how much authority over you a particular person has.

The next time you're confronted with a situation, ask yourself the following question: "In this situation or in relation to this person, is this a person in position to give me instructions? Or do I really have final say?" Some pre-thought will clarify for you a new awareness that will help you become more effective in your work and personal relationships. Instead of giving away final say about your life, you will retain final say in many situations. In addition, you'll regain control of your own life when you realize that there are certain situations when you are not in the driver's seat.

And Then You're in Control

So picture someone walking by as you are getting ready to pull into a perfect parking space. This person says in a bossy tone, "You can't park here. My friend is coming and I'm holding this space for him." I recommend you answer, "Thanks for the suggestion." In other words, you will react to this instruction as if it was a suggestion…and be clear in your own mind about who is really in charge.

(Of course, you'll adjust your behavior to circumstances. If you're in a neighborhood where each homeowner is allowed the use of the parking space in front of his house, where someone has the right to tell you not to park where you wanted to, that's not a time for "Thanks for the suggestion." Right?)

It's rather child-like to hear everything as an instruction and make adjustments from that limited perspective. Life can be better than that, but it's up to you to make changes. Just as a racquetball player who has played the game since childhood learns to adjust the distance she stands from the ball as she grows up and her arm gets longer, your ears and emotional muscles need to adapt in the same way.

Go slowly to stretch this muscle of hearing. Be clear about whom can give you instructions; it's time to stop and realize that you are in charge more frequently than you ever thought you were. I'm eager for you to recognize that other people behave automatically as if they are in control of you, when in reality they are not. It's up to you to make the distinction. Too many people feel overwhelmed by a world that seems to have taken over their lives. If you feel that you are only an insignificant cog in a wheel being powered by others, you will soon come to realize how much power you have given away. The exercises at the end of this chapter will clarify this important lesson and help you to stay in charge of your own life, which is another definition of Emotional Fitness.

If you let others inappropriately give you instructions, and if you don't give instructions when you're in a clear position to do so, your life will never come into balance—even if you meditate, do yoga every day or work out in the gym on a daily basis. You must learn to identify when you are in charge and when you are not. Giving up control in life can be compared to being deprived of vital nutrients; the primary emotional vitamin all people need is *final say*. Everyone—even children—must know the delight of being in charge of some part of his or her life. Most people recognize the importance of qualities like confidence and self-respect. But without clear areas of final say, there will be no lasting sense of self-worth.

Giving Final Say to Others

While you are learning the lessons in this book, I urge you to look at the people who are close to you, beginning with your family members, to be sure that each has areas of final say. With your children, I hope you will be sure that you expand the areas of final say as they grow. As a manager, let your direct reports know when they have final say. And as a significant other, help your partner develop and retain areas of final say in your lives together. That's the way you encourage people into Center Court with you. And then you can all enjoy the game of life together.

People without clear areas of final say become hostile, belligerent, combative and manipulative; they are the ones you often describe as "control freaks," needing everything to be done their way. Even serious troubles like anorexia, alcoholism and suicide can in many cases be traced back to a basic need for final say that has gone out of control.

People Have Trouble Taking Instructions...

Too many people who don't have clear areas of final say have trouble taking instructions. This is particularly true of young people. Too often, young people flare up when they're given an instruction by a parent or coach. I taught a class for teenagers recently, and when I put up the notice about a class in Assertive Behavior I expected to attract young girls, who are frequently curious to learn more about human behavior. But when the class met on the first day, I was surprised to face a group that included a number of young, macho, athletic males. I thought they had made a mistake and were in the wrong meeting room, but that was not the case. These athletes in lettered sweatshirts came to my lecture because they wanted to learn how to avoid getting in trouble with referees, coaches, teachers and parents.

Even they were tired of losing the fight for control, even though that was not how they described it. When playing soccer, football or basketball, they would often have a hard time accepting the coaches' orders. They would flare up and shout back, and end up getting benched or thrown out of a game. Even the pain of missing the game couldn't keep these young people from belligerently over reacting to an adult giving orders.

...Because They Take Too Many Instructions

Now why were these young people having problems? Adults have come to accept the reality that youngsters pumping new hormones typically reject and disagree with a parent's right to give them instructions. Most young people feel trapped in their own homes and in schools. They can hardly wait to make their own money and get free of parental control. Too often they want to leave home or quit school, and sometimes that's exactly what they do. Consider that these teen denials of parental authority are like the ones we find in the workplace—people having misconceptions about who can give them instructions.

But the situation is exaggerated for teenagers who take instructions from too many people. A teenager's life includes being given instruction by not only parents, teachers, coaches, store clerks, and almost any adult; but even from their peers—friends who really have no right to tell each other what to do. But the emotional clout that carries the fear of being rejected by his or her group causes the teenager to be saturated with instructions. The young person is clobbered all day with verbal and emotional pushing and pounding, and feels completely out of control. And all of this happens on top of the pressures that the hormones are exerting. Then along comes a coach or parent who clearly has the right to give instructions, but the youngster's feelings are worn thin and he/she can't take it any more.

Result? Explosion!

If today Dad has had a project taken away by a boss who needs to exert final say, Dad needs a control fix. Hopefully not by using alcohol or drugs, or driving home too fast; more likely by controlling his son verbally. And if, on top of that, Mom has had a similar situation at work, or been similarly controlled by waiting for builders or a repair service—you're looking at an explosive family situation.

Dad needs a way to deal with a controlling boss. Mom needs ways to handle the pressures in her life. And young people need to learn how to stay in the peer group of their choice while resisting the pressures. Saying "no" to peers or to bosses doesn't work. "Just say 'No'" does not pay off.

Saying "No" Is Very Hard

A young student was a very successful member of the debating squad, of which his French teacher was the director. The teenager decided that he didn't want to continue as a member of the squad, and told his French teacher that he wanted to play on the tennis team instead. But the teacher put pressure on him, saying, "I suggest you remain on the debating team." The young man thought this meant that his grade in French would suffer if he refused to take his teacher's "suggestion."

Did this teacher have the right to give the youngster an instruction about which outside activity to pursue? Clearly he did not. I was able to encourage this young athlete to stand up to the pressure and say politely to the teacher, "Look, I understand you want my experience on the debating squad. I really want to play tennis this term; but if you're up against somebody really tough, I'll come in as a back up. I want your support to help me do something that's really important to me."

He tried this. And it worked. He learned how to say what he wanted, and he made it happen. But most importantly, he learned that even teachers don't always have the right to give instructions.

In the recent past, I have had the opportunity to teach some Asian immigrants. Among the students were several men who had held important, responsible positions in their countries as doctors, lawyers or military officers. They had worked hard to attain their former positions, and had earned valuable experience that entitled them to respect and authority.

The loss of their homes and money due to political misfortune was, of course, devastating. But the thing I noticed most was that they seemed to have a sense of being deflated as human beings. Having once been used to giving instructions, they now felt that they were in a position of having to take instructions from everyone around them.

I was able to help these newcomers to the U.S. to understand that even though they might now be in a humbler position in society, there were still not that many people in this new country who had the right to give them instructions. Before I explained their situation to them in realistic, intellectual terms, they had felt obliged to comply with everything anybody who seemed to have authority told them. They were awed by anyone in a uniform until I explained that Americans who are not in the military do not take instructions from someone just because they are in uniform; that in the United States, there are not as many people to take instructions from as there are under other governments. Despite their modest incomes and humble homes, my students soon began to realize that they had remained self-determining human beings and had retained more control over their lives than they had thought.

In one exercise they became aware (amidst shy laughter and giggles) that Paul Newman had a list almost as long as an immigrant's when it came to who he had to take orders from. It did my heart good to see these newcomers to our shores sit up a little straighter.

Give Your Children a Chance to Say "No"

How often do you hear yourself telling your youngsters what to do? Do you ever say, "This is just a suggestion"? Many parents admit that by the time their children reach the age of twelve, they refuse being told what to do. This is a reality in our society—a reality that is neither pleasant to admit nor comfortable to live with. Some would go so far as to say it's a tragedy of our time and our culture.

I agree that it would be better if we were allowed by our children to teach and guide them through some of the difficult years they face from twelve to twenty-eight (which is an age that I have arbitrarily chosen from experience with my own children. The insurance companies choose an age to readjust high premiums when boys stop keeping the gas pedal down on the floor. I suggest you choose any age you think likely, but then add 10 years to what you expect.) There are too many situations where youngsters from every socio-economic group live without benefit of any parental support or guidance. Runaways, throwaways, latchkey kids and children of the well-to-do are all learning that independence and control is gained by money. So these children become smart enough to figure out ways of getting their hands on the money to buy themselves freedom from every variety of honorable adult control, power and final say. Unfortunately, too many youngsters discover dishonest and often-dangerous ways to support their need for freedom and final say.

For those parents who deeply desire to maintain some influence over their children, it would be a good idea to separate the words and concepts of "instructions" and "suggestions" starting when the children are very young. Children know what they want to eat and deserve to be encouraged to make many of these basic decisions even at a very early age. To bring up children with strong emotional muscles, parents would do well to request and suggest more often than order and command. I advise parents to give their children a chance to say "no" much of the time. If children are allowed to say "no" to a parent, they will one day have the strength to say "no" to their friends.

It's also important to make clear what areas of final say a child has—what to wear everyday except for holidays, what and how much to eat from what is served, (abandon the idea of "no dessert until everything is eaten"), colors and patterns for sheets and which friends come to the child's birthday party. Make your suggestions and make deals, but the kids have final say. Then when you decide to tell your child, "This is an instruction," it will stand out in contrast from most of your other "suggestions"—it will be viewed as rare and important and much easier to accept. Your child needs to feel a balance between suggestions and instructions, something I bet you never felt as a child. In too many homes, everything a parent wants a child to do seems equally important. This is why parents must give their children options, to ensure that they are not trapped as former generations were. And I believe that, should we do so, we will raise a stronger breed of independent thinkers. Perhaps this is how the nation will protect our fragile democracy and freedom—our youngsters will know better than kids of other cultures how to think and fend for themselves.

Don't wish that the good old days were back. See our culture as offering a better quality of life when each person is in charge of certain areas of his/her own existence.

Is It Really an Instruction?

Do you, yourself, take orders from too many people because you don't stop to consider if what you're hearing is an allowable instruction? If you drive into a parking garage in an aggressive part of any big city anywhere in the world, you'll surely get a lot of "orders." A parking attendant stands there yelling and waving his arms; "Come on, come on. Don't stop there. Pull your car up here. Leave your key in the car." Our world, unfortunately, provides many people who are overworked, underpaid and delighted with some authority to shout at you in doctors offices, hospitals, stores, garages, theatres, even at schools. (Yes, I met a controlling shouter at a university medical center only last week.)

But now that you're getting emotionally fit, I'd like you to pause and consider if this parking lot attendant really has the right to give you instructions. His /her voice may take on the vibrations of authority, and you may be cowed into believing he has the right to tell you what to do. His suggestion may even be reasonable, if stopping where it's more convenient for you has blocked other cars trying to get into the garage. But the attendant does not have any legal right to give you orders that you must obey. You may choose to allow him to be in control but please be sure it is your choice. You may be frightened, intimidated, or embarrassed, but you must not let yourself be driven out of Center Court. Elderly people often have physical pain and cannot park where an attendant says. Without complaining or begging, these people would do well to learn, while still vigorous, how to say what they would like to do. Everyone would do well to learn how to stay in Center Court under pressure from caretakers or people who try to intimidate them. Don't just assume that everyone is in charge of what you do.

There are coaches and counselors who would advise you to go out and change the world, demanding that people always do what you want them to do. Do not even think I'm saying that. What I'm teaching you is not to try to radically change the world but rather to be in charge of your own feelings and ideas—to be able to use the assertive skills appropriately. Demanding that people do exactly as you want all the time is an adult tantrum, not assertive behavior or emotional fitness.

So what are you going to do about this man shouting orders at you? He believes he's in charge of you, while deep inside you there's this new voice that says that he is not. The key to the way you respond is to first remind yourself, consciously, that he does not have the right to give you instructions.

So Who Can Give You Instructions?

As an adult, who do you have to take instructions from? How about the IRS? If an IRS agent calls and says, "Come down to my office," you'd better go, hadn't you? When the Highway Patrolman waves you over, you'd better respond. Government agencies are set up by society so we can all live together in relative order, so we've granted them the authority to give us instructions.

What about your boss at work? He has what we call clout because he can fire you and take away your income if you don't follow his instructions. A landlord can force you out if you don't pay your rent on time or don't follow the instructions of your rental agreement. If you're taking courses in order to get a certain degree or certificate, you had better follow the professors' instructions. You signed on to put them in the position of final say over your education; it's understood that you will only get the degree if you do things their way, according to their practices and deadlines.

Some people have the right to give you instructions because they have some power to impact your freedom or your finances or your future. There may be other people with a different kind of clout, like that of withdrawing love or affection (and by the end of this book, you will be able to handle those people who try to gain power over you with manipulative behaviors). But there are very few people who have the perfect right to give instructions to you. It's very important to your emotional fitness, and your emotional independence, to know exactly who those people are.

Make a List

So how do you avoid being browbeaten into accepting "instructions" from anyone who would like to give them to you? It's very simple. You make a clear and careful list of people who can give you instructions at this point in your life. It's pragmatically based on who has clout over you. Who can punish you in some way or make life difficult for you at this time?

You'll find there are not really very many people in position to do that. The telephone company is on the list, as are the electric company and your Internet provider. The list grows as you become trapped by your own desires. A close friend of mine rejects using many of the modern services simply because he refuses to be in the control of too many people. Freedom is his baseline for full contentment and, while I can only communicate with him via 'snail' mail, Emotional Fitness compels me to respect his beliefs.

Use the List

It's important for you to memorize the list you will put together, so that when someone comes up and shouts an order at you (and too many people have the tendency of talking to each other in terms of order-giving), the list will come to mind immediately. Then you'll think to yourself—"He's not on my list." Don't say it out loud; no need to be rude or antagonistic. Just flex your new emotional muscle.

Imagine that you go to the free outdoor concert, and an usher is telling everybody, "All seats in the last aisle." When he points towards that distant aisle, just watch everyone follow his instruction. He sounds as if he's in charge.

No, don't look at him and say, "Listen, mister, you're not on my list." Just think it; say to yourself, "This person is not on my list." Look at him and say, "Thank you for the suggestion, but I'd like to try the center aisle first."

You may believe that he's really in charge, that the management will throw you out if you don't listen to their employee. But you're wrong. The manager of the concert facility could ask you to leave if you do something disorderly, raise your voice or threaten to harm someone. But the bossy usher has no clout over you. He may wear a uniform, but he is not part of law enforcement or the criminal justice system. You probably would feel embarrassed not to follow along like a well-behaved, passive citizen; but when learning how to banish Anger and Fear from your daily life, you'll be delighted to find that ushers don't punch you, rattle handcuffs, or even make a face. What they usually do is simply let you to look for seats where you want to.

Let me repeat, when somebody tries to give you an instruction, make a quick mental check to see if the person is on your list. If not, tell yourself it's just a suggestion—and act accordingly.

When the chain goes up right in front of you at the supermarket check-out counter, that's a visual instruction that says "go to another counter." Well, I want you to see that chain in a different way—see it as a ribbon, as a suggestion. Don't respond automatically. Say to the checker, "I know that your shift is over, and you're eager to get off work. Would you be willing to find a way to process my order so I don't have a long wait?" Say it nicely and watch the magic happen. Again, I hope you will be mindful of basic rules of society. But miracles do happen. Something like this happens to me quite often; I ask a clerk to help me and he gets someone to open another register. My expectation is not that I should always get this treatment, but I am no longer afraid to ask—politely.

Your List Will Change

As you grow older, as you move from one area to another, or change jobs or activities, the list of people who can give you instructions will change. If you decide to sign your child up for soccer lessons, you're granting the coach the right to give her instructions and to have final say about what is worn to practice, language used and anything that occurs during lesson time. (Yes, teachers are clearly on your list of who has final say.)

Be honest with yourself. Do you take instructions from people who no longer have a right to tell you what to do? Have you retained your youthful "knee-jerk" reactions to the status of certain persons or authority? It may be that certain reactions are no longer appropriate at your stage in life.

Getting older is difficult for many people because those reaching an advanced age begin to get and take instructions from too many people. Like the child and the teenager, they find themselves without final say. When illness or weakness imposes itself on an elderly senior, and their families insist that they relinquish all decision making, depression often sets in. (As I write this book, I'm concentrating on how to assist elderly people retain some independence.) If you build your emotional muscles now and become emotionally fit, you'll be able to use them into your old age. Many elderly people never had strong emotional muscles, and like all muscles they are harder to develop as one ages

I know a man who had been in the military all his life. He had even attended a military academy as a child. When he was into his 70's and no longer in the service, he was still calling all the young men "Sir." I had a similar problem. I was raised to stand in respect whenever an adult came into the room. Then I passed the age of forty, an age that gave me permission to remain sitting. But I continued to stand when people who looked like adults to me would enter the room, and even sometimes for younger people who looked older than their real age. I've gotten over that now. Indeed, now is the time to grow a new group of muscles while we can, and make the needed adjustments to the way we feel and behave.

It's important to realize that you're in a different place in your life than you were as a child or young person. Make that clear list, and when somebody is not in a position to give you orders, be aware of it and don't respond just by following their orders. Too often following someone's orders will interfere with your doing what's best for you at the time.

By checking your list mentally before you respond to an instruction, you will learn how to slow down. Good. Slowing down to make sure your behavior is in your own best interest is a good thing. Very often it's quite possible for you to go right ahead and do whatever it was that you had planned or wanted to do. Just remember—if there's an official Police Department "No Parking" sign, then that's an instruction. But if it's just a hand-made "no parking" sign, you have a perfect right to ask for an explanation and decide for yourself if it's reasonable.

Give Yourself a Chance to Do What's Best for You

I went to a movie theater recently to see a very popular new film. My husband and I drove out to the theater with two friends who were visiting from the East Coast. We got to the theater early and discovered that a lot of other people had as well. My husband dropped us off to buy tickets while he parked the car. Taped to the box office window, we found a note that said, "6:45 show sold out. Buy tickets for the 9:15 show." Now this was forty-five minutes before show time. My friends were very upset and tried to run after my husband before he parked the car. Other people came up to the window and turned away when they read the note. I decided that there was another option, and I went up to the young lady seated behind the glass and said, "This is obviously a very popular movie. I was eager to see it, too. I've had the experience that there are always a few single seats left empty in the theater. I'd like you to make an exception and sell us four tickets." And she replied, "Sure. And if you can't find seats bring your tickets back for a refund."

Allowing for the fact that people are not perfect—and that the sign in the window was not an instruction, but a suggestion—I did not approach the ticket seller angrily. I understood that she had the perfect right to say "no" to my request, but I went ahead and did something that a lot of people wouldn't do because they were intimidated by the handwritten "instruction."

If you *demand* your own way, you are not emotionally fit—you're having a tantrum. By treating the no-tickets situation as a suggestion and making a quiet request, I was successful. That's the kind of delightful experience you can have when you're able to separate instructions from suggestions.

EMOTIONAL FITNESS EXERCISES

Part One

Instructions are *orders.*

Only a few specific people are truly in a position to give you instructions. Lots of other people may *act* as if they have the right to do so—by their tone of voice and the words they use—but they don't.

Some people *can* give you instructions.

It's important for you to be clear at all times about who really has the right to give you instructions.

A Sample List:

Who They Are	What They Can Do To You If You Don't Follow Their Instructions
1. The banks that hold mortgages on your property; credit card companies; service organizations such as the electric company, telephone company; etc.	Take away your property, credit, or service
2. The company you work for	Refuse to employ you
3. Government agencies, e.g., IRS, police, motor vehicles agency	Fine you, take away your privileges.

If certain people have emotional clout over you, include them in your list. Hopefully, you'll be able to cross them out by the time you've finished this book.

If you rent property, a landlord will be on your list; if you're taking courses for credit, a professor will be included. Be realistic about what they can do to you—don't over dramatize. At this time of your life, the people who have the right (and the clout) to give you instructions are:

Who They Are	What They Can Do To You If You Don't Follow Their Instructions

From time to time, the names on this list will change. Try to keep the list up to date. Also try to keep in mind, clearly and at all times, who is on this list. If anyone else speaks to you in the tone of an order-giver, **hear it as a suggestion.**

To end this part of the book, I have two questions with answers that may surprise you:

1. You are called to testify before a Congressional committee and a Senator looks down at you and says imperiously, "Just answer the question: Yes or No."

   Is that an instruction? Do you have to do as the Senator says?

2. A lawyer at a deposition hearing gets impatient and instructs you to hold your answers to a single sentence.

   Do you have to do it the way you have been instructed?

The answer to both of these is that, since neither of these situations comes under our country's Criminal Justice System, you can answer any way you like. It's different in a court of law. When a judge asks you to do something, you must do it exactly as you are told. This goes for instructions given to you by law enforcement officers, as well.

If you're unsure of some situations, think them through and get advice from an appropriate person, such as an attorney, who can assure you that you have the right to stay in charge of your own behaviors. Many people are learning to consider doctor's "orders" as suggestions and stay in charge of their own health, a very important sign of people using their own fitness muscles.

Part Two

Just as it's important to know who can give you instructions, it's important to know to whom you can give instructions. As I said before, it's good for everybody to be in charge of some part of his life. Don't let the chances you have to give instructions be wasted. It's emotionally fortifying to give instructions; it's the final-say 'vitamin' that insures confidence as surely as calcium protects bones.

A Sample List:

Who They Are	What You Can Do To Them If They Don't Follow Your Instructions
1. Your children; (remember, however, that after age ten, your clout is diminished)	Take away privileges
2. People whom you employ	Refuse to employ you
3. People on committees of which you're in charge	Ask them to leave the committee, or call for a committee vote to remove them

In marriage, couples can agree to take responsibility for certain areas and maintain the right to final say in that area.

Your list of people to whom you can give instructions:

Who They Are	What You Can Do To Them If They Don't Follow Your Instructions

3

Getting Out of the Anger Corner

Anger is a self-destruct mechanism.

A New Way to Serve

The next step in your journey is to build a very important muscle, the one that's going to rid you of your Anger. It begins with the learning of a very simple exercise, one that—like push-ups—needs practice. This emotional strength exercise will come slowly and awkwardly at first. But as you practice, it will become an integral part of who you are. It's an effortless skill that will keep you free of the burden of Anger. Then you'll be well on your way to Emotional Fitness.

Like any new physical skill—a new way to serve when playing racquetball, or even a change in how you walk—it's uncomfortable at first. It's natural to be tempted to revert to the old and trusty serve that could at least be counted on. But if you don't follow through and practice the new serve, you may never know the thrill of a truly dynamic game. Often, the people who muddle through the old way end up developing physical problems like tennis elbow. The correct way to perform any exercise will help prevent breakdowns and, in time, get you a markedly better game.

A Bright New Environment

Years ago, I worked for a time as a teacher of very young children at an inner city school. A brand new facility had been completed, bright and cheerful, with yellow walls and pale green chalkboards. It was fully insulated against the harsh street sounds and voices from the other classrooms. Everyone was thrilled about starting a new school year in well-designed surroundings. The teachers were confident that the children would learn enthusiastically in their ideal classrooms as the kids arrived in starched new clothes. The parents wanted their youngsters to be as perfect as they'd heard the new school was.

For the first week, everyone was delighted. But as the teachers and youngsters began to work together, the children became restless and unable to concentrate, not doing as well in their work as they had in the noisy, old, run-down schoolrooms of before. The teachers were puzzled; they couldn't figure out what was wrong. The children became irritable and their little voices became uncomfortably loud. The teachers blamed the administration; the administration blamed the teachers, and then started blaming the parents. Everyone was upset and angry.

I like to think that I have my own out-of-the box perceptions and remedies for problems, and I set my mind to examine the situation in hopes of finding a solution. I always figure that there are options and solutions to most problems that people don't always see, and as I thought about why the children weren't learning, I remembered an incident from my own childhood. Raised in noisy New York City, I had gone to spend the summer holidays in a countryside community in Canada. I remembered having had trouble falling asleep those summer nights because, as I described it, "the crickets were keeping me awake." The strange sounds of the country were making this city girl uneasy.

I had never been kept awake by the night sounds of the city; buses roaring past, cars honking, the shrill sounds of an ambulance were all my comfort noises—ones I had heard from childhood. There in the country I could not sleep because "the crickets were too loud."

It was then that I realized there was something off-putting for those children in the soundproof new school. To these youngsters, the tumult of a metropolis is comforting—it's home to them. They were not accustomed to the aseptic quiet of insulated rooms. So I brought in a record player and used Elvis Presley records as background noise. Soon the discomfort problem was solved and the children in my kindergarten class began to relax and learn. The teachers in adjacent rooms complained at the unaccustomed music, but my students calmed down and got right to work.

Now a question for you: Can you function without the noise of Anger and Fear in your life?

Anger and Fear Are Noise

Emotional Fitness will take away much of the noise in your life, and it may increase the brightness of every day. Fear and Anger are noise and produce shadows in your life. When your heart is beating wildly with the noise they create, your brain can't function at its best. On the other hand, if you've grown accustomed to the noise of Fear and Anger and the heartbeats of Anxiety, living in a quiet atmosphere might take some getting used to. But together we will work to take Anger away, and by taking it away, make your world a quieter and brighter place.

However, because you must continue to function during the transition, I won't eliminate the anxiety all at once. First I'll help you understand the concept that can remove your Anger. But then I'll leave it to you to absorb this concept at your own rate. The quiet will begin to settle on your life, and you'll gradually begin to get used to a life without Anger and Fear. You'll grow more comfortable and will be ready, as they say at the gym, to press more "weights." As your coach, I insist that you absorb what I'm teaching without losing any capabilities; it will surprise you to wake up one day and realize how emotionally fit you are.

I impose no time limits for getting rid of your Anger. As an experienced coach, I predict that you'll gradually rid yourself of Anger within about four or five weeks with only a minimum amount of thought and practice. You may break out in a little rush of Anger from time to time, but you'll be essentially rid of it.

If you have an extreme problem with out-of-control Anger, you are in the wrong fitness class. A savvy physical fitness coach does not give a guarantee that fitness can be achieved in weeks, regardless of your initial physical condition. In the same way, although you have no release paper to sign, this program does not substitute for an intense program in anger management. I would not guarantee that the approach you're learning here would work for O.J. Simpson. For the rest of you, simply read on and relax while you learn the very simple concept and exercise that will get rid of your Anger.

Now Get Rid of Your Anger

There was a time when actors, writers and creative artists of all kinds thought that their creative juices came from Anger. Many people of artistic bent were afraid of learning to live without their old fears and phobias and angers. Samuel Goldwyn once said, "anyone who sees a psychiatrist should have his head examined." It was another of the laughed-at Golwynisms, but too many people harbored that feeling of fear of having their productive, creative juices dammed up by growing up. Little did they know that the *memory* of Angers and Fears would be data points they could call on forever, but that as adults they could live better lives without anxieties ruling their lives and relationships.

Every now and again I still meet someone who says that Anger is good, and that it's important to feel it and show it in a positive way...whatever that means. That Anger could be a good thing is like telling a teenager acne is a good thing because the poisons in the body are leeching out. Believe me, you want to get rid of something that causes distress to your body and to relationships and work, and that's what Anger does. It is a fertile ground for illness. It deprives you of the chance to live an effective life. Anger clouds clear thinking, and even clogs creative juices. So let's work to take Anger away. Soon you'll be closer to spending most of your time in Center Court.

The Ideal World, the Real World, and the Word 'Should'

In order to understand how Anger operates in your life, I want you to realize a basic difference between the ideal world and the world you live in. First of all, let me explain that I am an idealist. I aim for the stars and I prefer to think of the world as being beautiful and polished and kind and lovely. But we all know that the world isn't always perfect. Emotional Fitness Training is meant to be training for effective behavior in the real world, the world of everyday living, regardless of these maddening imperfections.

If you go to a college campus, or if you're invited to participate in a planning group, and you want to talk about how the world *should* be, you can use that word and you will have my blessing. You'll aim for the stars and dream, without considering any reality. It's a beautiful world, and you want to make it even better. That's a wonderful sort of conversation to have, and 'should' becomes your philosophical hitching post.

But the word 'should' is one word I want you to discard for any real world situation. You will experience Anger whenever the word is brought into everyday life—whether you actually say the word out loud, or you hear it uttered in your presence, or you merely sense and feel its pressures. I'm sure you can remember someone shaking his or her finger at you and saying, "You *should* arrive on time," "You *should* ask directions when you're lost," "You *should* take notes instead of trusting your memory." We were all brought up with that word, because that was the way our parents brought us up as children.

'Should' sets a trap for yourself and anyone in discussion with you. Research shows that when you're trapped, you get angry. It's a reaction of nature. Your pulse races, your body prepares for "fight or flight." You get angry whenever your options are taken away— and the word 'should' is the word that traps you back in the Angry corner of the racquetball court. I would like you to become very aware that the word 'should' in real-world activities is a word that traps you, robs you of options and drives you into the corner of Anger. If you go to the Brookings Institute one day to plan how the world 'should' be, you can plan and daydream at the 'should' level. 'Should' is a beautiful word for planning and discussing ideals but, again, does it have any meaning in the everyday world we live in? No, none at all.

And of course, the corollary of 'should' is 'shouldn't.' "You *shouldn't* keep me waiting," "You *shouldn't* be embarrassed to ask for directions when you're lost," "You *shouldn't* think you can remember everything without taking notes." Throughout all the following, everything I say about 'should' applies equally to 'shouldn't'.

Pack 'Should' Away...

I would like you to take 'should', wrap it up, and pack it away. You can pull it out to use at a think-tank, or in church, or when you're on a planning committee for your town. I hope you'll get out there and talk about your dreams and how the world "should" be. But that's where it ends. 'Should' is a planning word, a mental word, but it has nothing to do with everyday functioning.

...And Live in the Real World

What substitute words for 'should' fit into real-world thoughts and actions? To continue along the path towards Emotional Fitness, I suggest that you substitute the words, *"It would be better if...."* When you see a banana peel on the street, instead of saying, "People *shouldn't* throw banana peels on the street," substitute, *"It would be better if* people didn't throw banana peels on the street." Instead of saying to a child who has come in the front door covered with mud, "You shouldn't come in here like that," say, "It would be better if you came in the back door when you're all dirty like that."

Each time the word comes into your mind, I want you simply to change the 'should' to the reality phrase.

Arynne SIMON SAYS

'SHOULDS' are not part of the real world. Emotional Fitness is "reality behavior."

Even seemingly harmless 'shoulds' add up to anger and stress at the end of the day. They take away the options and keep you out of Center Court. Keeping aware of your 'shoulds' will help you get rid of your Anger…and fast. As you learn to accept the reality of the world, your Anger disappears.

How Does It Sound in Center Court?

A manager in a well-respected high tech company used 'should' on his direct reports all the time. He had 'shoulds' about how his engineers should dress, about what kind of voicemail messages they should leave, and about how they shouldn't come in even one minute late to any meeting. He may have been right, but his people didn't stay long enough to learn from him. He switched to "it would be better," and kept his people and helped them to learn. His career has been on a roll since that first lesson he was able to absorb.

A male student of mine had created a serious problem in his family because of his inability to control his Anger when he drove the car anywhere with them. He would get so angry because of other people's driving mistakes, that he would rant about what the other driver's 'should' and 'shouldn't' do, and upset his family to the point that they refused to go any place with him. As the result of Emotional Fitness training, he learned to replace his 'shoulds' with "It would be better if…." His attitude toward other drivers gradually softened, and he became more tolerant as his Anger was displaced. The car became his training "vehicle" for many similar behaviors in his life.

A woman student's specific problem was the Anger she felt whenever she walked into her children's messy room. When she would see the clothes and toys spread all over the floor and beds, she would accuse the children and fight with them over being orderly. Her Anger seemed endless. As she learned to substitute, "It would be better if you picked up your room," for "You should keep your room neat," she slowly became less angry and more effective in influencing her children's behavior.

Yes—I know it sounds simplistic, too easy to really work. But it *does* make a big difference. Give it a chance.

Other Words That Trap You

There are some other words that also mean 'should' that you also want to look out for: 'must,' 'ought to,' 'have to,' 'got to.' For example, instead of saying, "I *must* get my work done," say, *"It would be better if* I got my work done." And so on.

Remember, when you use a word in the 'should' family, you're getting Angry; and when someone uses a word in the 'should' family to you, you know they are Angry, and you will soon be Angry as well.

As you grow aware of how you're actually talking, you may find that you often don't speak three or four sentences in a row without a 'should'. "I *should* call him." "I *should* finish that report today." "I *should* make plans for the weekend." And when you meet a friend on the street, you even say, "We *should* get together for lunch." As you stop and repeat each statement with a substitute "would be better if," you'll feel as if you're tripping over your tongue. This won't last long. It will soon feel natural to you.

At this point, a student might question what good this simple change of one word can do. You may actually be surprised to see your stress level begin to drop, even if you don't even trust what benefit you might achieve. Your doctor may even notice a change in your heart rate from the use or non-use of the word.

Arynne **SIMON SAYS:**

Don't say to yourself, "I shouldn't say *should.* "
Instead say, "It would be better if
I didn't say *should!*"

EMOTIONAL FITNESS EXERCISES

Eliminating your 'shoulds' is a simple exercise, so it may be hard for you to believe that you're going to get rid of Anger merely by getting rid of that one word. But it works. For now, I suggest not worrying about the underlying reasons because I know you're impatient for this to work.

Get rid of all 'shoulds', and in just a short while you'll feel your Anger receding. There are no pills to take and no family secrets to reveal. If it seems too easy, I can promise only that old habits are sometimes tougher to break then you imagine. Just watch out for 'shoulds.'

1. Finish the following sentences. Then repeat them out loud substituting "It would be better if" for the 'shoulds.'
   A husband/wife should always ⎯⎯⎯⎯⎯⎯.
   Children should ⎯⎯⎯⎯⎯⎯⎯⎯⎯.
   Teachers should ⎯⎯⎯⎯⎯⎯⎯⎯.
   Car dealers should ⎯⎯⎯⎯⎯⎯⎯.
   Mothers/fathers should never ⎯⎯⎯⎯⎯.
   Television should ⎯⎯⎯⎯⎯⎯⎯⎯.
   The government should never ⎯⎯⎯⎯⎯.

2. Make a list of all the 'shoulds' and 'shouldn'ts' you use during the day. ⎯⎯⎯⎯⎯⎯⎯⎯⎯⎯
   ⎯⎯⎯⎯⎯⎯⎯⎯⎯⎯⎯⎯⎯⎯⎯⎯
   ⎯⎯⎯⎯⎯⎯⎯⎯⎯⎯⎯⎯⎯⎯⎯⎯
   ⎯⎯⎯⎯⎯⎯⎯⎯⎯⎯⎯⎯⎯⎯⎯⎯

3. Make a list of all the 'shoulds' and 'shouldn'ts' you hear during the day. ⎯⎯⎯⎯⎯⎯⎯⎯⎯⎯
   ⎯⎯⎯⎯⎯⎯⎯⎯⎯⎯⎯⎯⎯⎯⎯⎯
   ⎯⎯⎯⎯⎯⎯⎯⎯⎯⎯⎯⎯⎯⎯⎯⎯
   ⎯⎯⎯⎯⎯⎯⎯⎯⎯⎯⎯⎯⎯⎯⎯⎯

4. Make a sign and place it by your telephone, "It would be better if...."

5. Choose one area of your life you're particularly angry about, and start to practice applying the "would be better if" language when you talk and think about it.

4

It's All in the Wanting

Arynne **SIMON SAYS**

You are what you want.

Wanting Brings People Closer

One of the most important steps you can take toward becoming emotionally fit is to *want* things…and to know *what* you want—to be aware of everything you want. To want things is to be in touch with who you are. (But, again, to demand that you get *everything* you want is a tantrum.) Telling others what it is you want gives them a chance to know who you are; you don't get to truly know others unless you take the time to find out what's on their "want list."

Conversely, by not telling people what you'd like, you're pushing others away. Parents often buy clothes or gifts for their children and discover they were wrong in what they selected. Young people, as they strive for privacy and independence, often go through a long phase of being unwilling to openly share their wants with their parents. Some adults also wall themselves off in a similar way; a child asks his father for a Christmas or birthday gift suggestion, and the parent answers, "I don't want anything except for you to be happy." That places a huge burden on the child, who would find even an expensive sweater easier to give.

The capacity to want a lot of things, and to keep on wanting all through your life, is a good way to determine one's Emotional Fitness. In a very real sense, each of us can be described and defined in terms of what we want. During the sixties, many young people wandered from one side of this country to the other—searching for their identities, looking for themselves, wondering who they were. In actuality, an identity is most accurately mirrored in the things you want, and in the way your Wants List changes as you yourself change through the course of your life. To some extent, you can even keep in touch with the changes happening in your inner self by staying aware of the changes in your list of wants.

Though this may seem like a materialistic attitude, it is most certainly not. It is just a simple and fast way to know who someone is. Surely you've had the experience of cutting out an ad for a book, a tool, a computer gadget or a trip. You've tossed it on your desk, and then even a week later you wonder why you bothered. But while a lot of our wants seem frivolous on reflection, we all have many that have stayed steady over the years. Getting in touch with your wants is a simple way to stay in touch with who you are and who you were.

But it's necessary to be constantly aware of the changes, to perceive how your wants evolve and develop as you grow and change. As you browse through a catalog or magazine or menu, you are, in a way, figuring out who you are right now.

Material Wants Will Lead to Deeper Understanding

I suggest that the simplest way to learn about yourself is by realizing and understanding the material things you want—things that carry price tags. From these superficial wants you will eventually be able to describe the other things you want out of life, like career goals or family goals, and even your own description of a contented life.

But I want you to begin thinking about material wants, and to express these wants to others in a light-hearted way. The ability to express what you'd like in tangible terms is like having a series of handholds to grab onto as you climb a sheer cliff; though reaching them may be difficult, each one you do reach helps you along on your journey up the cliff. It's very difficult for most people to allow themselves to express wanting anything, so I suggest you start with very small material wants and work up, gradually, to those more difficult emotional and spiritual ones. I predict that, by doing the exercises, you will soon be able to say things like, "Some day, I want to be important in my community. I want people to know who I am and what I've done." This is the kind of ultimate goal you might come to express as you grow emotionally.

Successful people are able to put their wants into words, and some are even able to request that others help them to achieve their goals. Think of political campaigns, or leading the local chapter of a major volunteer organization.

Start with Small, Unimportant Things

The worst fate that can befall a person is to look out into the world and say, "There's nothing I want out there—nothing I desire." This is often the plight of older people, which causes intense discomfort for their children, who see in these words the expression that life is over.

Men, in particular, find it difficult to share what they want with others. They don't like to shop for ordinary things that might give them pleasure; it's considered less manly and materialistically superficial. Many people disdain the catalogs that come in the mail. Perhaps you are a person who is not willing to spend any time flipping through them. But my term for these catalogs is "wish books." Think of them like that. The whole idea is to find yourself amongst the tools, the lamps and the jellybeans packaged in decorator boxes.

But to begin, I'll suggest you start by getting in touch with some very small things that you want. A hobby, for instance, gives a person a chance to identify some of their wants. A man who becomes a fishing enthusiast gets a sense of himself by wanting certain items, like a new fishing accessory, or wanting a chance to learn fly-fishing. Suddenly people know what kind of gifts to get him; he doesn't mind going into a clothing store, because he's always looking for a new hat that might do for fishing; and soon fishing magazines begin arriving at his house. Now this man can be described partly in terms of something that others know he wants; he comes alive to his friends because of a simple hobby. The fisherman is often described by those who know him in terms of his love for the sport. This human being now has a facet that shines, and everyone around him enjoys the reflected light.

At the end of this chapter are exercises to help you identify some small wants. As you begin to know that you want a certain kind of PDA or comforter or compass for your car, try to remember that I'm laying the groundwork for your getting to know the deeper things you want—the important things that will build quality into your life. Please don't be impatient while you proceed to emotional fitness step by step.

Take Advantage of Gift-Giving

It's important to understand that, for many reasons, people are often afraid to get close to each other, or to know someone too well. Gift giving is a chance to get to know others better. A person who is a good gift selector is perceptive and picks up the small signals that others give him. He proves to those he cares about that he understands who they are by giving them things they want.

Give others what they would like to be given. The old nugget of buying a gift that you'd like is surely meant to parallel what we were taught by the Golden Rule. But a gift is a perfect chance to know someone else and delight that person with your choice. It says, I know you and I like you—just as you are. Do not consider gift-giving occasions as some commercial trap set out by American business. Gifts are a way to enjoy the benefits of getting close to others—a way to think about others and define them according to their wants.

Arynne SIMON SAYS:

You know people better if you know what they want.

What someone wants at a particular point in their life is a clue to who they are and how they feel. Children go off to college wanting subscriptions to *Seventeen* Magazine, and may enter their second year asking for a subscription to *The Economist*. Pay attention if you have a daughter whose Christmas list suddenly includes things for a kitchen rather than just makeup or clothes.

On the Receiving End

Of course, gift giving works in both directions. I'd like you to begin letting others know who you are by saying such things as, "I used to read fiction all the time, but now I'm fascinated by biographies;" "I never cared for the Rolling Stones much, but I heard a tune the other day and want to start collecting their CDs;" "It's about time I got a scanner for my computer but I don't know where to go to find out which is the best one."

If you consistently say, "I always get the wrong gift—nobody really notices me," maybe you're not letting people know about you. Maybe you are keeping your distance. And think about the office situation: if a manager never gets reports on time from his/her team, maybe it's because that manager never states exactly when he/she wants to receive them.

I had an experience standing in a gift-wrapping line in a department store recently that illustrates how little we know about those closest to us. Two young men were also waiting in line to get packages wrapped, and one of them said to the other, "You know, I bought my father bookends. Every year I end up buying him something that has to do with books—bookends, a book, an empty book to write in. I don't know anything else my father has ever wanted." The friend responded, "All I ever buy my father are pipes or tobacco—something to do with pipe smoking." Both these fathers had permitted their sons to get only very limited views of who they were. It is, indeed, a sad reality.

There are people who have no more idea of what would please another person close to them than those two young men did—and it's not all the gift-giver's fault. Most people are embarrassed to say what they want, and in a very real way we set each other up for failure by not expressing our wants.

At this point, I'd like to warn you to be patient and not immediately go out and start telling all your friends, relatives, neighbors and co-workers what you want. First of all, I'd like you to finish this chapter and the following one before you begin expressing your wants out loud. If you begin before finishing the two chapters on wanting, you will not be aware of all the concepts involved, and your wants may come out sounding like demands—which, as you'll see, is what causes many people to shut themselves off from expressing wants.

Once you've accepted the role of letting others know your wants, your goal will be to keep adding to your Wants List, and then learn how to appropriately describe your wants to others. This two-part skill of knowing what you want and having the courage to tell others is a big step in getting emotionally fit.

...But Don't Change Your Wants into Needs

It's important not to change the wanting into *needing*. When you're a jogger, you strive to keep a jogging pace, keeping in mind a clear sense of the distinction between walking and jogging. They are different actions, using many of the same muscles but in a different way. Most people can readily learn to distinguish between walking and jogging. But distinguishing between *wanting* and *needing* is much harder for most.

Rethink Your "Needs"

Right now I'd like you to think about what you *need* to have today, or what you *need* to do. What kinds of things are on your need list?

Make a list of the things you need to do or buy today.

NEED TO DO

1. _____
2. _____
3. _____
4. _____
5. _____

People often list such things as 'needing' to buy a birthday card, 'needing' to have some office supplies ordered, 'needing' to call a business friend for lunch. Others list 'needing' to write a business letter, 'needing' to go to the post office, to make some telephone calls, or to find a rental property for a client.

Words Are Like Boomerangs

Let's examine these 'needs.' Begin by recognizing that the word 'need' implies something essential for you to have success or achieve a desired goal. It's important to realize what pressure you're putting on yourself when you say or think you *need* something. Words are like boomerangs. You think you can just toss them out into the air, but they come right back to you and can trap you. If you say that you *need* to make a certain phone call—then you imply that there is going to be trouble if you don't. When you say that you *need* to meet your wife for dinner, you're trapped. You've taken the pleasure out of what was supposed to be an enjoyable. If you *needed* to come home from a business trip with a gift for your little girl, then where's the fun of shopping for it and giving it to her? If you *need* your tennis racquet restrung, where's the satisfaction in getting it done before the next club tournament? You're putting stress on yourself just by using the word, and putting yourself out of Center Court.

Needing Usually Means Wanting

There are a surely a few things people need, but most of the items on a typical Needs List are items that could go without getting done for a while. Most families could go without grocery shopping for the next three or four days and still have enough tuna, noodles, canned soups and frozen vegetables—whatever—to serve up adequate meals. Going without a birthday card, a gift, or a lunch will not do much damage. The Needs List would best not include even getting the racket restrung because, while it would make the game more fun, you could manage without. Right?

However, these could all belong on a Wants List. And that's what most of daily life is all about. Wants that you translate into needs unnecessarily trap you; recognizing a want for what it truly is frees you from that trap. At home, I have a pad that has "NEED TO DO" crossed out. "WANT TO DO" is substituted. Make one of these pads for yourself. (I hope you *want* to do this. because it is surely not something you *need* to do.)

The phone calls you *want* to make are important for you because you want success, and the rental property you *want* to find for a client is important to your work—but even they are not *needs*. The birthday card and the restrung racquetball racket are important to your joy in pleasing a friend and in playing a good game—but they are not *needs*. By saying 'need,' you take away your options. And unless you life is one with options, you are without the ability to live without stress.

[Helpful Hint: Men who *need* sex are not as much fun as men who *want* it. Most women don't appreciate the stress factor added to sex. Men who *need* sex rather than *want* it are trapped by their own needs.]

Will People Hear if You Say What You Want?

As children, we were conditioned to believe that there was something selfish about expressing what we wanted. Therefore it became more acceptable to say, "I need…" That made the desire legitimate. As a youngster, if I had wanted a pair of shoes because they were what my pals were wearing, I probably never could have just come out and said that. To my parents, it would have sounded spoiled, a waste of money.

Baby boomers may have a different sense of how money was spent on them, but to children raised during the 40s and 50s, we didn't get what we wanted unless we could rationalize it into something that was needed. So you might have claimed that your old sneakers were too small, that you trip because they are too worn. You might even have limped around for a day or two in order to convince your folks that those new shoes were really necessary.

Your thirteen-year-old tells you he *needs* some new running shoes, when actually he really *wants* some new ones because the old ones are not the latest, cool style. A man says he needs a new car; he complains about every squeak his car makes and gripes about gas mileage or whatever he can dream up. But he really wants a hot new design to gain the envy of his buddies. A tennis player sees a new model racket and all of a sudden he's not willing to use his old one. "I could get tennis elbow from this heavy racquet."

It takes a special form of courage to come out with a forthright statement like, "Gee, it'd be great to have one of those new racquets. I absolutely don't need it but I sure want to one." Assertive language is honest, without excuses, and unafraid. It is NOT aggressive. It doesn't include 'shoulds,' 'yous,' or 'gottas.'

It is aggressive behavior if you hear too many 'shoulds' and manipulative rationalizations given to justify preferred actions. People who are not emotionally fit transform wanting something into needing it in order to get permission to do what they want to do. It's curious and sad to see how even nurses and doctors, involved with serving serious needs, are very likely to put a false kind of pressure on each other. I taught some of the staff at a nationally famous hospital, and was struck by the way the intensive-care personnel talked to one another— applying stresses far beyond the real pressures of their work. Everything was described at a *need* level— use of the phone, dispatching of orderlies, calls for charts and documents—everything. The personnel were burning out fast. They felt extreme tension that went far beyond the inherent pressures their emergency work generated. Both doctors and nurses passed their stresses onto the suffering patients.

I worked diligently with the hospital staff to help them separate the words 'want' and 'need,' and taught them to use 'need' very sparingly. Within weeks the entire atmosphere changed to one of less pressure and less intensity, and more smiles began to crack through—a measurement of success and relief for everyone. In addition, the work was done more efficiently because people felt like cooperating and helping each other. Harmful sounds and angry pressures were lifted, and the patients benefited from the improved atmosphere. A few of the patients were told about the training I was giving the nurses, and also discovered that if they asked for help using "I want" or "I would like" rather than "I need," they were more quickly attended to.

You know the story about the boy who cried, "wolf!" We make the same kind of mistake every day by improperly crying, "need."

Time to Reverse the Process

So to insist that you try living life from Center Court, I'm going to take the word 'need' away from you for the time being. In place of the word 'need,' I'd like you to use the word 'want'—until it becomes so automatic that, if you happen to go to the hospital, you'll be able to tell the emergency room doctor, "I *want* a blood transfusion!"

Eliminating unnecessary occurrences of 'need' from your everyday vocabulary will give you the freedom to play life from Center Court, where success, effectiveness and a delight in living are found. In order to get there and stay there, you'll do without the word 'need' until you're able to use it only when it's *needed.*

EMOTIONAL FITNESS EXERCISES

1. Start a "Want List" or file folder that can hold clippings or memos about things that you want to buy, learn, visit, and do. Or keep an I WANT folder on your computer desktop. I have one that includes books I want to read, people I want to invite to parties, and recipes I want to try. As you evolve and change, you can update this file to keep it up to date with who you are. Remember—your list describes who you are at any given point in time. When you look over your earlier lists, you'll be amazed at how much you have changed.

2. I suggest that to start, you can organize your Want List in terms of how much things cost.

   Start with items that don't cost anything, such as: a day by yourself to putter in your workshop or browse through art galleries; guaranteed uninterrupted time to read or watch television; breakfast in bed on Sunday morning; time to take a leisurely walk.

   Things that cost under $10—a paperback book, a new pen, a magazine, a new mouse pad.

   Things that cost from $25 to $100.

   Things that cost from $100 to $1,000.

   Things that cost a great deal.

3. See if you can describe yourself from your Want List. If this were a stranger, how would you size up the person based on the list? Where is that person headed at this point in his/her life?

   One woman told me that she looked back into her Want List and found it filled with kitchen gadgets. Now that she is divorced, she's substituting make-up, perfume, and clothes. And some great books for long evenings alone.

   Remember the important lesson from this chapter: a good day is a day when you know what you want, and have the courage to say it out loud. Remember, too, that this doesn't mean a good day is a day when you can *get* everything you want. By now you are beginning to understand the importance this difference makes. Assertive behavior, always misunderstood, is about having the courage to request what you want, not about demanding to get what you want—which is aggressive behavior.

5

Do You Have
a Perfect Right?

**Although you have a perfect right to
ask for what you want, you don't have
a perfect right to get what you want.**

Waiting to achieve something is the antithesis of the "Now" generation. The baby boomers grew up believing that wanting and getting happened in the same timeframe. In terms of being emotionally fit, most people have no muscles to support the reality that 'wanting' and 'getting' are as different from each other as baseball is from swimming. It would have been better had you been taught to put a wide chasm between wanting and getting. This is another essential part of becoming emotionally fit: accepting the fact that, just because you can't have something, doesn't mean that you must stop wanting it.

As you become emotionally fit, you will learn to put 'wanting' and 'getting' into proper alignment. Consider the delight of the courtship period before marriage, when two people grow close in spirit and take pure delight in each other. Both talk freely about the things they want. As they drive along on a Sunday afternoon, the woman might say, "Oh, look at that great house on the beach! I'd like a house on the beach so I could walk the dog each morning at sunrise." Her boyfriend might also dream out loud, "Someday I want to design a house; maybe one of those ecologically correct houses, or a real modern all-glass one." They drive on a little farther and she says, "Look at the boats. Someday let's have a boat." He says, "I want a sailboat. Maybe we'll sail around the world. Maybe we'll go to France one the summer and take canal boats all over Europe. Would you like that?"

They use this language of courtship to get to know each other by sharing their dreams, their wants. But since they're not married, he doesn't feel obligated to buy her dreams for her, nor does she feel any obligation to satisfy his. Courtship is about getting to know each other, and each is free to speak. Listening comes easily without any obligation.

But what happens after this pair gets married? One Sunday they take a drive and she says, "Oh, look at that gorgeous house, honey." He turns to her and says, "If you wanted a house like that, you shouldn't have married me. I'm the wrong guy—I'm not going to make that kind money for twenty years, so forget it!" As a married man, he's starting to hear differently—and he's starting to feel obligated to supply what she wants. And these days, with so many wives holding jobs, this works in both directions.

Too often, they both stop listening—and so stop knowing each other as they evolve. She doesn't want to hear what he wants; sex, dinner on time, a party for his friends, or an arts-and-crafts-type house instead of the modern one he wanted a few years earlier. The willingness to hear each other, such an endearing quality during courtship, is shrunken to nothing.

The confusion of 'wanting' and 'getting' is the killer of far too many relationships, and responsible for the too-frequent complaint that "no one listens to me anymore." Marriage doesn't have to be the end of a happy communication about what each one likes and wants.

Traditional Concepts of Wanting

Too many girls are raised with the idea that if they want something, it will be their husband's duty to supply it to them. Men, too, are raised with the idea that if they want certain pleasures or certain pampering, they have a right to count on them being provided. And both men and women also absorbed the notion that, once a man became successful, he would give his wife and children everything they wanted. These days many children, too, are growing up with the idea that it's their parents' duty to provide them with whatever they want. People have been led to believe that if they express a want, they have a right to get it, especially within the family group.

Though it seems a contradiction, it is nonetheless true that the society also teaches that it is spoiled and self-centered to want. I remember a particular Christmas morning when my daughter's pile of presents looked like Mt. Everest. She would open a gift and spend time playing with it and enjoying it before opening another. Finally I told her the remaining ones would wait until after she had a nap. She went up to her room for a rest and watched some TV. Soon after, she bounded into the room, tripping over her many new toys, and announced: "Mommy, mommy, I just saw a new Barbie on TV and I want it so much!"

I understand that your immediate reaction might be one that most of us would have gotten: shock and annoyance, followed by angry words that would include selfish, spoiled rotten, etc. "Look at that heap of presents you just got, and you're asking for more! What's the matter with you? I don't want to hear any more about what you want." And then comes the tirade against the TV commercials that push toys onto our kids.

That kind of explosion comes from feeling obligated to provide what your child wants. Parents try so hard to please the children, especially at Christmas. The complains make parents feel unsuccessful, because they're not able to fulfill every want. Blaming the child and TV is how this is too often handled.

ARYNNE SIMON SAYS:

Sharing your wants
is sharing yourself.

Now let me tell you how I'd like you, if you're a parent, to respond in this kind of situation. If you're not a parent, please learn nonetheless from the essence of the example.

When my daughter bounded into a gift-filled room and told me that she just saw a new Barbie doll and wanted it, I smiled at her and said, "Oh, it would be wonderful to have that doll! It sounds even prettier than the one you opened this morning from Aunt Gladys. Please remember it for Valentine's Day if you still want it!"

I did not interfere with my daughter's expressing what she wanted. I shared her excitement and hope, but felt no obligation to get this Barbie doll for her.

I knew she wanted it, and we may have even shared some excitement talking about it again the next day. But I had no intention of doing anything more about it.

Nowadays my little girl is grown up and wants to travel to exotic places, a stable with a barn hand, some fine hunter/jumpers and regular visits from a trainer. She wants many things and says so. Does she expect anyone else to get them for her? No. Does she work for them? Yes.

But the important thing is that I continue to know my daughter through her expression of what she wants. And she knows what I want, although I'm not as good about expressing these things as she is. Our daughter has also learned to postpone getting what she wants. She can live within a budget. Best of all, she understands that wanting and getting are not always part of the same timeframe.

This concept requires a two-way responsibility: with one person expressing what he/she wants, and the other listening without feeling any pressure. Over the years, I have heard from married men and women that the weekends are the toughest days of the week. Added to the many chores are the voices of their loved ones expressing wants at various intensities, and expecting that the wants will be fulfilled. The "Honey-Do" list ("Honey, do this; honey, do that") is not funny. It is an expression of what someone wants that the other *must* do.

Learning to Say "I Want" without Putting Pressure on Anyone

As you have already learned, it's extremely important to know what you want and be able to say it. Now you're about to discover how important it is to be able to say your wants in a way that doesn't exert undue pressure on another person to satisfy them for you.

Think about your own behavior. Do you *demand* rather than want? You demand when you assign someone else the burden of giving you what you want. This demand/instruction behavior is clearly appropriate in business by bosses, managers, or someone in charge of an event or project. But for most of life, it's emotionally rewarding to live with *suggestions, requests,* and *wants* rather than with *instructions, demands,* and *needs.*

Go Ahead and Say It

As an emotionally fit person, you're learning to say out loud and unembarrassed what you want and what you'd like. "I'd like a glass of water, with ice in it." Or, "I'd like a house on a hill with a private pool and Jacuzzi—inside." Learn how to feel free to say what you'd like—because you have a perfect right to want things. But when you express your wants to others, be sure they sound like *wants,* not *expectations*—dreams, not must-haves.

How to Keep in Touch with Your Family

It's very sad when family members grow apart, but it's never really too late to bring family members closer together. Even if you have grown children, or old friendships that have grown stale, you can begin to speak or write to them about the things you'd like to have; about the things you want to learn, read, do; about places you want to see or even a job you'd like to have. Remember that when you stop wanting things, there's nobody there to relate to—nobody can know who you are. You become dull; you grow old. People are at a loss to know what to give for gifts; they don't know what will please you. They don't even know what to talk about with you.

Relationships in business, too, are built and expanded, and become more satisfying, if you take time to ask questions and get others talking about what they want out of life and work.

Set people up to succeed.

When you let people know what you want, and help them to be successful in pleasing you, life becomes better for everyone. Before holidays, a birthday or anniversary, I encourage you to mention the gift you'd most like—so that the person who might buy a gift for you will be able to please you with something you really want. Don't wait to be surprised and, perhaps, disappointed. If you find that you habitually return gifts, then consider if the problem might be yours for not helping with suggestions. If you think "they should know what I want by now; they should know my favorite colors and my taste in jewelry, clothes, food or wine," then you're setting people up to fail you. (It's also possible, of course, that you're surrounded by people who don't listen.)

If you think that people who care about you should "read your mind," then you're probably not only disappointed regularly—you're also not living in the real world. You may be the kind of person who listens and remembers how people drink their coffee, and you may remember what people say they collect, what things they've mentioned that they wish for. You may be good in that way, but most people are not. It's unrealistic of you to expect that kind of attention and keenness of observation from others.

Too often, I find myself in the position of reminding wives to set their husbands up to be a success before a birthday arrives. "My birthday's coming up. If you have in mind buying me flowers this year, I'd like lavender flowers. Lavender in anything is a new favorite of mine." Try not to be embarrassed to speak of what you'd like. It's much more fun to let the people around you succeed for you. And saying that you find lavender becoming a new favorite is a fun way to describe that your tastes evolve and change. Good for you!

Go through Life as if You're Shopping with a Friend

It's worthwhile to think about two young women shopping together. One says to the other, "Look at that dress! Wouldn't I love to have that for New Year's Eve!" The girlfriend replies, "Oh, wouldn't that be great! Imagine, if you got red shoes to go with it and wore some of the new Dior make-up!" The friend is right with her, dreaming and planning and wanting. Compare this interaction to that of a mother and daughter as they shop. If the daughter says, "Look at that dress! I'd love to have that!" The mother responds, "What do you need it for—you have two others in black." There's no chance for the daughter to enjoy the wanting experience; she's discouraged and told how foolish it is to want. The mother hates to hear her daughter dream because she feels that a walk through a store is a burden on her budget and emotions. The mother hasn't learned to listen without feeling the obligation to satisfy her daughter's every dream.

So, I'd like you to go through life as if you're shopping with a friend. People often wonder why they're closer to friends than to family. Well, it may be because we don't feel obligated to do or buy anything for our friends. And when near a friend, we have a chance to express our wants without burdening someone else. It's up to you to get as close to that attitude as possible with your family, especially your spouse or significant other. Encourage them to tell you what they want and what they like. If they don't seem interested in what you want, keep saying it. Keep telling them until they finally figure out what it is you're all about, and that they have permission to do the same with you.

Or better still, leave this book lying around, open to this section.

EMOTIONAL FITNESS EXERCISES

1. Postpone buying things you can afford, at least until you've taken the time to write them on your Want List. You will increase your pleasure in getting something if you take the time to want it first—by saying it out loud, or putting it on your list. Don't short-circuit your pleasure by giving up wanting.

2. Tell those close to you what's on your list. Even children can please you by buying for you as gifts the small things on your list such as a magazine or a can of tennis balls.

3. Make a list of the things you want that you will probably not get for some time, or that you may never get—a house over-looking the Mediterranean, a world cruise, a fine art collection. These are things that you can read about, dream about, and talk about. You may never actually get them, but they can provide you with much pleasure nevertheless.

4. Share the concepts you have acquired with your co-workers, your boss (if appropriate), your husband, wife or significant other. Begin to talk freely about what you want, making sure that the people in your life know they're under no obligation to get or do these things for you.

5. From time to time, review the idea that a good day is a day when you stay in touch with what you want, and have the courage to tell someone. "Boy, I sure would like to be in London at the British Museum." Then get back to whatever you were doing, feeling better for having shared your want out loud.

6

Building Your 'No' Muscle

You have a perfect right to request anything.

Part of becoming emotionally fit means learning to get some balance into your life—another way of describing Center Court—so it requires learning to say 'no.' But before you can say 'no' to others, you must first learn to take 'no' for an answer. You are about to work on building your 'no' muscle.

The Man Who Couldn't Say 'No'

Continual research is part of what a professional does to be sure that what we teach is accurate and valid. So when I was living in Washington, D.C., one day I decided to do some research to check on a concept I was teaching and writing about.

63

Early one morning, I went with notepad in hand to a small shop in Georgetown. I had been in the shop before, and vaguely remembered the man behind the counter. That early in the morning, I was sure there wouldn't be much change in his cash drawer So I went up to him and said very casually, "I'd like to have change for this $10 bill." He looked up and said, "Oh, gee, I don't think I can—that'll use up all my change." I said, "Okay, it's not important." And he said, "You know, I really don't have it." I replied, "It's really all right," and I walked to the door and just stood there looking at my notepad, perfectly relaxed and unperturbed. He called out from behind the counter, "You know, if I had it, I'd really give it to you." Again I calmly reassured him and repeated, "It's all right; it's not important." Suddenly he darted toward the back room shouting, "Wait a minute! I think I have it in my coat pocket in the back. I'll be right out!"

It's Very Difficult for People to Say 'No'

When faced with saying 'no', people generally react in one of two ways. We either say 'yes' because we're too uncomfortable about saying 'no;' or we do manage to say 'no' (often indirectly), and feel really uncomfortable about it. When you're asked for help—to give money to this charity or collect for that one; chip in for a gift at work; spend a weekend on a help-the-homeless project someone at work has organized; lend a hand with a project for church, school or a political group; take care of a neighbor's child—and you want to say 'no,' what frequently comes out of your mouth instead is 'yes.' You feel trapped.

You're not in Center Court when you have lost touch with what you want. If you do manage to say 'no' to protect yourself, you probably feel guilty about it. When President Reagan's wife Nancy introduced the "Just say No" campaign, I wonder if she realized that she was asking young people the emotional equivalent of competing in an Olympic gymnastic event—without being trained.

If you want to learn to use your 'no' muscle when it's appropriate, that's fine. You don't want to be trapped by the fear of a grudging 'yes' or the anger of an aggressive 'no.' You want to have the ability to say 'no' comfortably and without feeling guilty. But it's always better to know what you want.

Give People a Chance to Say 'No'

Assertiveness courses are given, and books are written that purport to teach how to say 'no.' But none of these methods teach how important it is to be able to hear a 'no' from someone else and to accept it. It's my opinion that until you can comfortably catch a 'no,' you will not have the emotional fitness necessary to pitch a 'no' to another person. Unless people are allowed to say 'no' to you, consider that you have some flabby emotional muscle tone—and it's time you firmed it up a bit. The flexibility in giving and taking negative responses is an intrinsic measure of emotional fitness.

A skier who attempts a steep slope with locked knees is headed for trouble, and can expect that every mogul will put him off balance. The unbending person who expects always to get what he wants will find life as precarious as a ski run iced over with dangerous moguls. There are times when it's perfectly appropriate for people to tell you 'no.' It's essential that you learn to identify and accept those 'no' situations.

One of the nicest gifts you can give another person is the opportunity, the space, to say 'no' to you. If, by your attitude, you can show people that it's all right for them to do so, you take the pressure off them, relieve their anger and fear, and put yourself in a much better position to build a positive relationship with them. Have patience. Sooner than you think, you'll be amazingly effective in getting more 'yes' responses—especially when you really want them.

Building Your 'No' Muscle

The way you're going to learn to accept 'no' from other people is by doing a series of exercises designed to get you a 'no' answer. You'll learn to use a certain kind of effective language that may be very different from what you're used to when asking for things.

These exercises may be quite difficult for you to do at first. But as you gain more practice, you'll get stronger. Eventually, these exercises may even be fun to perform. They are your warm-up exercises, just as a dancer does barre exercises before getting out on the floor and a runner does stretching before heading out. You'll always be able to keep yourself in shape for effective behavior by performing these activities. They're part of the inner structure of Emotional Fitness.

Every "no" you get is like $1,000 in the bank.

I'd like you to envision every 'no' you get as a $1,000 bill which you will deposit in your 'no' bank account. As your bank account increases, you'll grow in emotional flexibility and strength. And when the time comes for you to say 'no' to someone else, you'll have plenty saved and ready to spend. There's not a chance you're going to be able to say 'no' comfortably until and unless you have this 'no' bank account. The sooner you get out there and start asking for things that you don't need or even want, the sooner you'll begin to develop the Center Court balance that will allow you to gracefully accept every 'no,' and eventually be able to say 'no' comfortably.

A Sample Exercise

To give you an example of how the exercises will work out in practice, I will describe a situation that illustrates the techniques and kind of language you'll use, and what you can expect for results:

You are going to ask a passing stranger for change for a dollar.

You approach a stranger who is passing by and ask for change for a newspaper or a parking meter. You're not going to give an explanation or any excuses like, "I'm late for a doctor's appointment and I've got to have a quarter, or I'll get a ticket." Just make the simple statement and rely on your voice and the words to make your request. Look at the person gently, don't get so close as to be threatening, and say, "I'd like change for a dollar."

Make a request with a statement— not a question.

It will probably be difficult for you to make this request with a statement rather than a question. It seems much more natural to say something like, "May I please have change for a dollar?" Or, "I'm sorry to bother you; can I ask if you've got change for a dollar?" You might think that you'll sound like a spoiled child when you say, "I'd like change for a dollar." But I can assure you that those are the most rapidly understood words, and if your attitude is casual and undemanding, they are the words that will get your message across more effectively.

'I want' and 'I'd like' are phrases that communicate honestly and directly. With some practice they'll become more comfortable, and very soon they will seem natural to you. Let me remind you again that a good day is a day when you know what you want and have the courage to say it out loud to someone. Anyone.

This simple exercise takes courage. Many people give excuses that seem to make sense to them, but I know they're just afraid to try asking people for anything—even more so when it's something they don't really need. Remember, the answer you're trying to get is 'no.' Try to relax, and simply depend on the straightforward language.

By using simple, assertive language, you may sometimes get a 'yes.' But once again, the purpose of the exercise is to get a 'no' answer. So when a passerby says, "No, I'm sorry. I don't have it," your response will be, "Okay," or "All right," or "No problem." You're not going to ask a second time, and your relaxed reply will assure the other person that it was okay to say 'no.' Remember that this stranger is probably finding it difficult to say 'no' to you. Keep trying to get the 'no's you need for your bank account.

It might help to get your courage revved up if you convince yourself you're just doing some research. Also, make a mental note of the various things people say or do to avoid saying 'no' directly, like making excuses or jokes. Congratulate yourself for every 'no' you get.

It's Your Attitude that Counts

Your tone of voice and, most importantly, the attitude that people do have a right to say 'no' to you, are reflected in the language you use. Many grandparents (and not a few parents) think it's bad manners when a child says, "I want a glass of water," instead of "May I have a glass of water, please?" They find this assertive form of expression to be offensive. Despite what many people think, *please* and *thank you* are not magic words. Consider the possibility that it's not the language by itself that's important, but the building of a new, softer attitude of acceptance. What you're learning is not just about the words of assertive behavior, but about the attitudes as well.

So which form is appropriate for children to use when requesting something? Think for a moment of French or Spanish (or most other languages): there's a familiar form of speech, and a polite form. In the same way, I think of "I want" as a familiar form for children to use, and "May I please" as a polite form. To a grandmother a youngster might say, "May I please have a glass of water," but to her parents she may use "I want..." The appropriateness of the language is easily understood by children when it's explained to them. They adapt quite well—just as children can learn to hold doors open for older people, even if they don't for their friend.

The "Center Court-ness" of Emotional Fitness opens many opportunities for you to be gracious and kind. I would like to suggest that you not reply automatically with the words 'thank you.' 'Thank you' does not suit a moment when you have just gotten a 'no;' they are not words that are used to patch over a hurtful moment. Use them precisely, as words that are like gifts you give to others. And since 'thank you' is not a complete sentence, I suggest you finish the sentence when you do choose to use them. Not just 'thank you,' but rather, "Thank you for asking me to give you my opinion," or "Thank you for inviting me to be your guest speaker," or "Thank you for holding the door open for me." The world will be a more elegant place if we begin to use a very special phrase and a complete sentence as a reward when someone does something really very special for you—when someone says 'yes.'

The other night at the movies, a woman who had arrived late stepped over a whole row of feet to get to an empty seat against a far wall. Instead of saying "excuse me, excuse me, excuse me," she said "thank you, thank you, thank you," for helping her find a seat in the dark. In a very real sense, each person had done her a small favor, and her 'thank you's were a gracious and noticeable pleasure to hear. I looked to my left and to my right and saw smiles on all the faces in the row. Everyone was in Center Court.

EMOTIONAL FITNESS EXERCISES

Listed below are a number of suggestions for building your 'no' muscle. In each case, the aim is to make a request that allows the other person to say 'no.' The idea is for you to learn to accept a 'no' comfortably and gracefully.

Just say, straight out, what it is you'd like. For example: "I'd like change for this dollar, please." If the answer gets you your change, respond with a "Thanks." To any other response, answer with "All right" or "Okay."

The effective language for this exercise—

Women: Use the words 'I want' when you are making a request to a stranger. Use 'I'd like' with family.

Men: Use 'I'd like' for all your requests. However, if you are normally very soft-spoken, use 'I want.'

Young people: If you're younger than mid-twenties, use 'I'd like.'

- RELAX
- DON'T TURN ON THE CHARM
- DON'T GIVE REASONS
- SAY SIMPLY WHAT YOU WANT WITHOUT PUTTING PRESSURE ON ANYONE ELSE

The Exercises:

1. Pay for a newspaper, mints, or anything else that costs less than $1, with a $5 or $10 bill.

2. In a drug store or supermarket, request change for a $5 bill without buying anything.

3. Go to a restaurant or fast-food place, say you're not eating there, and ask for a glass of water.

4. Ask to use the rest room in a store where you are not a customer.

5. Go to a gas station that has a full-service island. Ask the attendant to check the air in your tires or the water in your radiator, or ask him to wash your windshield, without buying any gas.

6. Ask the checkout attendant at a supermarket for six small bags or other extras.

Remember—Be sure to choose an appropriate time to make your requests, a time that is not too busy for the storekeeper or clerk. The goal is to get people to say 'no.'

BUILD A BANK ACCOUNT OF 'NO'S. WHEN YOU HAVE A LOT OF THEM SAVED UP, YOU'LL FIND IT MUCH EASIER TO SAY 'NO' TO OTHER PEOPLE. YOU'LL BE STRONGER WHEN YOU CAN ACCEPT A NEGATIVE RESPONSE.

NOTE:

Some people resist these suggested exercises. "Isn't it unkind to practice on people who are bushed and busy after a long, hard day of work?" I agree. That's why I suggest that you make your request at an appropriate time or when a sales clerk isn't busy. There are lots of things you can ask for without putting people out. Some of the suggested exercises may be too difficult for you at first. Just go ahead and do the ones you can. Later, with more emotional muscle tone, you'll have greater strength and the ability to return and practice the harder exercises.

Also keep in mind that the end result of doing these exercises and developing your 'no' muscle will be to make the world a better place. People who get 'yes' answers all the time have a sense of being out in Center Court by themselves. If others don't have the right to say 'no' to you, you're playing a lonely game.

I measure how emotionally fit I am by the number of 'no's I get. As a girl growing up in New York City, I learned how to get my way and all the 'yes's I wanted. But I know now that the truly successful, together person is the one to whom people can say 'no.' It's important to play the game of life so that others can give you a good rally, and to realize that assertiveness combined with kindness does not take away your ability to be really effective when it's important to you.

7

Breaking the
Golden Idol of Feelings

ARYNNE **SIMON SAYS**

Everyone's tears are salty.

I say, "Hooray." In recent years there has been a growing respect for the virtue of intuition, and for people to believe that their feelings are as important as their brains. Feelings are generally accepted and openly expressed in many aspects of private and public life.

But has it gone too far? Celebrities shed tears in front of television cameras on interview programs. Politicians tell us their "feelings" about important issues. Businessmen are less embarrassed to talk about how they 'feel' things should be done. In personal relationships, family groups, and encounter sessions, people have been led to believe that it's necessary to "let it all hang out"—to display their deepest emotions. And "how do you feel" is a question reporters ask whenever they can.

It's true that much emotional damage was done when a person's emotions were held in control and never expressed. Now that feelings and emotions are expressed almost indiscriminately, it's my view that the pendulum has swung too far. Emotions expressed without precision do not benefit anyone; emotions inappropriately expressed can, indeed, be quite harmful. Anger management is different than anger control; emotional management is far different that emotional suppression or denial.

At the end of the working day, many confused people complain of being overworked, blaming their tiredness on constant phone calls, interruptions by their boss or co-workers, and the unfairness of many company policies. But it's not the work that wears people out. Most people are emotionally flabby, really tired from constant interruptions of Anger and Fear, keeping themselves out of Center Court during the work day.

As you're learning in this book, emotions are best expressed when you want to use them, when you consciously decide that the situation is appropriate. You are in charge of when your emotions are to be activated—and in charge of being sure they don't just take over. Recall the story about my daughter and the water faucets from an earlier chapter. Little children have trouble remembering which faucet is for hot water; they get confused and turn on the hot water when cold was what they wanted. A grown-up knows which is which. But when it comes to emotions, a lot of people turn on the emotional hot water faucet because they haven't learned how to adjust their feelings. And so we allow our emotions to be abused.

The emotionally fit person possesses the same range of emotions that belongs to all humans. But he/she has learned which faucet to turn on, and when. None of us want to become intellectual, mechanical robots, or go back to the days of suppressing our emotions. Leaning the methods of emotional fitness means that work—whether paid or volunteer—becomes less tiring and more satisfying. Home and work each have their own optimum mix of intellect and emotions. Until you're emotionally fit, you won't be in charge of the mix.

It's time to begin to use your intellect to add definition and precision to your emotional expressions.

Feelings Are Manipulative

The word 'feeling' is intended to express your emotions. But it has too often become a way we intentionally or unconsciously manipulate others. When you're over-reacting or raging out of control, your voice is hooked up to your feelings. People use language as a weapon; and when you express your feelings with sarcasm or quiet anger, you brutalize other people. And they often don't even know what's happening to them. Some feelings are so powerful when they're expressed that they wound others, especially those close to you. Your angry words create ugly scars.

It would be better to handle emotions, quietly, when you're alone, perhaps writing them down. I don't mean to deny or squash your emotions, but rather to accept them without fear that a negative feeling might last forever. I want you to learn to feel your anger, accept it, and trust that time will relieve its intensity. It's really not necessary to *express* your feelings in actions or in words. It would be far better to handle your own feelings and express your wants.

People in the business world, politicians, radio and television personalities and leaders of every sort, would do better to let their feelings pass through their brains, and only then express a well-formed opinion as an idea, not a feeling. Wouldn't it be a relief to hear a leader say, "I've decided after thought and study that this nation should do thus and so," rather than, "I feel we should do thus and so." Who needs leadership that is emotionally based!? A calm, reasonable conclusion expressed as an experienced opinion is much more conducive to clear-headed planning and productivity than hot, confused emotion.

Often your intuition and feelings will have become an intrinsic core of an idea or conclusion. But how much more effective you could be if you learned to express your conclusion as a result of thinking things through. When I hear a politician say how he 'feels' about an issue, I conclude that perhaps he hasn't worked long enough or hard enough on getting his feelings integrated into his ideas or separated from his conclusions. Perhaps this leader is, indeed, trying to evoke an emotional response rather than a thoughtful, carefully considered one. Many charismatic, emotionally charged leaders lead people's brains into the jungle where they are in danger from poison-tipped arrows.

Emotions are beautiful and natural, but clutter up clear thought. When a speech appeals to sentiment, direct thinking is impeded. And so at fundraisers, the best speakers are people who know how to tug at the heartstrings. The separation of feelings and ideas as much as possible in the working world will make for greater professionalism and success. To solve problems, I suggest using the heart and brain in private. Then use your intellectual voice to deliver the decision you have made.

Feelings are mighty powerful. People are more willing to disagree with your thoughts than they are to disagree with your feelings. If you truly want people to be free to express their ideas to each other, even if they don't agree, you will express your ideas and conclusions in a laid-back style. Who was it that said that you have a prejudice, and not an opinion, if the back of your neck gets hot when the subject comes up? By eliminating the word 'feel,' you don't eliminate your feelings; you simply allow others more freedom to disagree with you.

I once heard an especially confused educator from Washington, DC, say on a television interview, "I *think* I *feel* that my *opinion* on that subject is..." This was one mixed up lady! While you're still feeling something, you have not yet put your opinion together. Emotionally fit people can wait until the idea is fully formed before expressing themselves.

Women and Men and Feelings

I wrote in the Introduction how my mother, a one-time suffragette, ended up believing in her later life that women had no place in business or politics. She was unable to define exactly what the problem was with women in the working world, but she said they were "mucking it up."

I think that what she meant—because I have seen it now for myself, after many years in the business world—was that women habitually expressed and showed their emotions; crying if they were criticized and 'loving' the new carpet that was chosen for the hallways of her office building.

Historically, women worked for a while, then decided they were too tired to cope with both work and home. They stayed home a while, then tried again. They ran a zigzag career course. My mother noticed that women in her day lost their tempers, expressing in emotional terms their opinions on situations that would have been better served by the use of facts, data, and logic. It was true then as it is now, that many behaviors are inappropriate in the working world and better left at home.

Very often a husband, remembering the emotional strife of his wife's previous job, says to her, "I don't want you to go back to work." She replies, "I promise I won't get involved this time." But six or eight weeks later, there she is with her undisciplined emotional muscles giving way to the problems and personalities at work.

Women tend to make friends with work associates and get involved with the relationships between people. A woman at work tends to use her emotions more and more as she turns the workplace into a home base. Soon she starts coming home too tired to share in the emotional life of her family, and uses her brain to organize her home life. Some women begin to sound like a drill sergeant at home and a nurturing parent at work. Home is where the emotions are meant to be active; work is meant to be primarily about the brain. And of course it's not just women. These days many men, as well, overuse their emotions at work.

My mother had liberal, humanistic views, and my father was a conservative Republican. She provided him with her emotional, intuitive input on issues; he incorporated her feelings into his ideas and policy making. The final decisions were made intellectually, but had their roots in warm feelings. My mother, the product of another age long gone, didn't believe that women had a right to go out into the world and spread their emotions around. She may have marched for women's rights, but she concluded that emotions belonged at home where they could privately influence thinking. High emotions are best not employed as problem-solving tools.

Until very recently, women were more comfortable with their feelings than men. Men tend to depend on intellectual evidence and, unless they have had some counseling, are short on the ability to examine their feelings. The two paths converge to make a total approach to a problem. With greater knowledge and awareness, every individual, male or female, is capable of acting on the stunning combination of feeling plus thought. This emotionally fit balance is the ideal that all people would do well to aim for.

Talking to Children

Even with your growing children, it may be better to use ideas rather than feelings when asking for their cooperation or understanding. Your feelings will tend to be accepted by those who love you without the need to understand them. Your intellectual conclusions require understanding.

Children at all ages perceive more freedom to develop their own opinions and make their own decisions when a parent describes ideas in an intellectual way. If a parent tells a child that he 'feels' the child should do something, the child is pressured by the fear of hurting the parent's feelings if he decides to ignore the suggestion or request. So I suggest expressing your thoughts and requests in the intellectual form. Only then will you be able to confidently say that you don't control your children.

My mother taught me—and her thinking on the subject of child rearing is quite old fashioned now—that it was a mother's job to give her children an accurate emotional language. Lucky for me that she described the feelings I had before a school debate as excitement. She never described them as nervousness. So to this day that rush of adrenaline I feel before a speech is, in my mind, excitement, not nervousness.

ARYNNE SIMON SAYS:

The word precedes the feeling.

In many families, little attention is paid to the development of conversation in which each participant is free to express individual ideas and listen to the ideas of others. Even young children can surprise us with a different outlook on a subject that we no longer see with fresh eyes and an open mind. Instead, in too many households, as soon as a youngster voices a slightly differing approach to a subject, he or she is quickly put on the defensive. The 'different voice' is silenced by disdain and disapproving grunts, or perhaps a joke or snide remark. The subject is changed, or talk simply dwindles away.

Despite all the news and the fascinating information constantly beamed at us, many still tend to talk about the same things repeatedly in order to avoid controversy and discomfort. How boring!

One of the Worst Examples: TV Panel Shows

In an ideal world, the smarter, more verbal people of any society would set patterns that the rest of us could use as examples. And to some extent, that's what happens.

But not on television. From TV discussion programs that feature media celebrities, we can watch and learn the skills of the most dysfunctional kind of discussion techniques. The talkers are shouters, and their facial expressions show complete disrespect for a disagreeing point of view. In my opinion, these discussion shows are the truest form of violence on American TV. I'd rather a child of mine watch a shoot-'em-up film than see the fine art of discussion butchered by news pundits.

People stop listening when they're frightened or angry. Their brains turn off—they are no longer rational. When a conversation turns to a controversial topic, Anger and Fear can produce put-downs, threats, and more. People refuse to listen to the opinion of others; they rarely admit that any position is right except their own. When did you last hear someone say in discussion, "That's an interesting point; I never heard that said before"?

The Social Conversation

The rules are different in the social setting—a gathering at home, dinner with friends at a restaurant, a pick-up conversation at a favorite bar, and so on. Too often, unless we know we're with people who all think more or less alike on important topics, we make a point of avoiding incendiary issues (religion, politics, and the like—even, in some circles, favorite sports teams) because we're afraid somebody will take offense and the conversation will become overheated.

Having an argument break out might be a hostess's worst nightmare, worse than charring the steaks. Much safer to stick with topics that are completely safe, the same topics you talk about all the time—maybe how expensive everything is these days, or what you did last night, or where you might possibly think you may want to consider maybe going for your vacation.

Again: Borrrrring.

Once you have mastered the skill of learning to express your thoughts instead of your feelings, you'll begin to discover that social occasions offer a splendid opportunity to hear differing points of view. Perhaps you will even have a chance to learn something new or change your mind.

Remaking Your Language

Because feelings are very beautiful, ephemeral things, they're best saved for quiet, special times with special people. It would be better not to overuse them and abuse them in the noisy outside world. It's more effective to use ideas, and give others the space to disagree with you and say 'no' to you. So what I'd like you to be able to do is talk about politics or any other controversial topic in a way that doesn't put you into the corners of Anger or Fear, and doesn't put anyone else in those corners, either.

Actors cry on cue, writers meet deadlines, surgeons perform operations. People who want to succeed in business and in their personal lives want to be that professional. The illustrious John Barrymore was once asked by a director to cry for a particular scene in a film. He asked the director, "Out of which eye and how many tears?" Living life professionally does not mean without feelings. It means being in charge of your feelings.

Aggressive, manipulative behavior doesn't allow people to use their brains. It pushes at their Fears and Anger. When you make it clear to someone that their ideas are worthless or ridiculous, that's aggressive behavior in its worst form. Parents and bosses do that to the people closest to them. I perceive it as an unfortunate kind of emotional abuse.

Because feelings are too tender to expose in public, and are only appropriate with those we care about, I have a new way of behaving that I want you to start learning. Would you be shocked if I suggest not using the word 'feel' in public?

Arynne **SIMON SAYS:**

As long as your thought remains a 'feeling,' it's not a clear expression of an idea. Consider that exposing your feelings in public may be a form of indecent exposure.

The word 'feeling' is manipulative. If you say you 'feel' a certain way about something, it implies that if someone disagrees with you he's going to hurt your feelings. Rational decisions cannot be made or carried out if people are operating at the feeling level. The word 'feeling' is therefore inappropriate in business and politics, and often even at home.

So I would like you to learn a new way of speaking. Rather than saying, "I feel like going to the movies tonight after dinner," you're going to start saying, "I'd *like* to go to the movies tonight after dinner." Instead of telling a worker, "I feel like you aren't trying hard enough," which is not only making an emotional statement, but isn't specific enough to let the person know what it is you want of them, simply inform them that "I want that report on my desk before you leave today."

Remember, Emotional Fitness means encouraging other people to get into Center Court with you. Saying what you 'feel' drives the other person into a back corner.

You are being coached to live a better life. Enjoy the process. Master the skill of speaking from the intellect, not from your feelings, by doing the following exercises.

EMOTIONAL FITNESS EXERCISES

1. Write a request for money to benefit a worth cause without expressing any feelings.

2. Frame three sentences to tell a child, husband or parent that you were disappointed at being forgotten on your birthday without adding any heavy emotional content—no guilt, no shame.

   If they feel compelled to say "sorry" when you're finished talking, you may have failed this exercise unless you have prepared in advance something to say that will reassure them. Hint: Talk about next year and tell them you'll send a reminder. Have some fun with this one.

3. Someone has sent you an email with a very different opinion than yours. Write the words you might use to tell them your appreciation for being shown another point of view.

ARYNNE SIMON SAYS:

Remember—you don't have to flash your feelings; everyone knows you have them.

8

Fear Is a
Four-Letter Word

ARYNNE **SIMON SAYS**

When you win, nothing hurts.

Walk Hand in Hand with Fear

There are a number of fears that all people share. These very human fears are ones that have become the core plot lines of literature and drama through the ages, as well as the theme laments of poetry and song lyrics. The greatest one of these is the inescapable fear of death, both for ourselves and for the people we care about. Death is a part of life that we don't want to occur, even while knowing it will eventually happen to all of us.

Among the other leading human fears are rejection or a forced separation from someone we love, and the threat of dishonor or acute embarrassment. These universal conditions are difficult for most people to accept with any calm. Illness or injury with no hope of full recovery is a fear we share; the very thought of being incapacitated and dependent, of being disabled or disfigured, unable to lead independent lives, is unthinkable. And the fear of unrelievable pain is also in this category.

Bankruptcy is another fear that many Americans share, although people who have suffered through severe financial setbacks and recovered generally do not include bankruptcy when listing their fears. The majority of immigrants who come to our shores without material possessions or money confront the economic strains of beginning a new life as just another of life's challenges.

But a great many Americans have never known extreme deprivation, or been challenged with extreme economic tragedy. Even the idea of moving from a four-bedroom apartment to a two-bedroom, or giving up a big luxury car for a smaller, fuel-economical model, can be perceived as a disaster by citizens of this great land.

In the United States, we spend the smallest percentage of personal income for food in man's history, but we continue to complain about the high cost of food when checking out at the supermarket. Losing wealth has become an all-American fear, as has aging, being fat, or being single or childless. These fears may seem superficial to citizens of other nations, but Americans are delighted with their advantaged lives and prefer to live that way. Therefore the list of fears may be longer for our citizens than others who have experienced tragedies and pulled through.

That walking hand in hand with fear—learning how to cope— had better be a goal for people who aspire to emotional fitness.

Arynne SIMON SAYS:

A 'catastrophe' is any event that dramatically changes the course of your life.

'Fear' is NOT the Same as 'Catastrophe'

If you accept my definition of a catastrophe, then you'll agree that only some of the above mentioned fears should be categorized as catastrophes. Getting a smaller car would not change the course of your life since you could still work, drive the kids to little league, or drive to the emergency room of a hospital, should that be necessary.

So if an event changes your life only in an insignificant way, it doesn't qualify as a catastrophe. For example, if you have a fire in your garage when no one is home, that's not a catastrophe. You don't have to move, insurance will probably cover your losses, nobody was hurt. You can go to work tomorrow morning, even if you have to carpool with a friend or take a bus or train.

But if your house burns down, that qualifies as a catastrophe. You will have to find a new place to live; family photos and many items of great emotional value may have been destroyed; and the course of your life will change as you spend weeks buying new clothing, looking for a new place to live, dealing with the insurance company, and all the rest.

The amazing thing is that when a real catastrophe occurs, most people handle the realities of getting on with life pretty well. Friends and relatives rally around to help, and the stricken family or individual discovers hidden strengths and rises to challenges, often with amazingly brave and even noble actions.

Catastrophizing

There is, however, something many of us do that causes us unnecessary pain. It's like tearing a muscle and finding that just this one muscle may keep you on crutches for a month or more. Perhaps a better description is using the metaphor of referral pain—when, because one muscle is injured, many surrounding muscles are used inappropriately. Soon the pain is located far away from the original center of stress.

Emotional muscles get stressed in the same way when people interject imaginary fears, what I call 'what if's, and perceive these as catastrophes. The exaggerated dramatization of *possible* consequences is what I term *catastrophizing*. Unfortunately, it's a thought process we were trained to excel at by parents who were trying to protect us from the many 'pitfalls' of this huge and unfair world.

I have found that people are attracted to their favorite catastrophes. To one person, every squeak in the night is a rapist; to another, a bounced check short circuits to fantasies of a jail cell; a letter from the IRS means instant bankruptcy; a spider produces images of extreme pain, paralysis, a wheelchair, even death. Because these tendencies to catastrophize were learned in early childhood, the individual doesn't realize how rapidly one gets from problem to fantasy, how we drive ourselves out of Center Court into the corner of Fear.

Arynne SIMON SAYS:

When your fear is an *accurate* emotion, recognize it and deal with it.

Don't Go out in the Rain

Even the most seemingly innocuous examples of this behavior can turn from a Woody Allen-type of exaggerated scenario to beyond Kafkaesque before anyone realizes. Here's a funny and typical illustration of catastrophizing:

One dark, cold, rainy morning, a ten-year-old boy is about to leave his house when his mother stops him. "It's raining—wear your galoshes," she says; (this was a long time ago; today she'd say "overshoes.")

He replies, "No, I don't want to."

She says in a louder tone, "Just put them on."

He says, "I don't want to—they make me look like a baby."

His mother warms up to the argument, "You'll catch cold. And it won't be just an ordinary cold—you'll get pneumonia, and you won't get over that very quickly. You'll get so sick that you'll have to go to the hospital. You'll have to miss a week's worth of school, and you're doing so bad in History that you'll never catch up; you'll have to go to Summer School." (She's getting him worried now as she threatens sickness and isolation.) "It's not easy to be in the hospital, but that's where you'll end up because you didn't listen to me. And if you think I'd take care of you so sick, you're mistaken. I'll send you off to the hospital by yourself." (Now she's adds possible rejection.) "And while you're in the hospital, they'll give you all kinds of painful treatments, and I'm not going to be there to fight for you—

no way, because you didn't listen to me." (Pain and helplessness is added.) She comes in for the finishing blows. "You can die from pneumonia." (Death.) "And when my friends ask me, 'Why did you let him go out without galoshes?' I'll be ashamed because you dishonored me and made me look stupid." (Dishonoring the family—worse than death.) "Then after you die and we get through paying all the hospital bills, we'll be bankrupt!" (Poverty and all that goes with it.)

Guess what this ten-year-old wears to school on that rainy day.

ARYNNE SIMON SAYS:

Some people manufacture their own misery by catastrophizing.

Who Really Suffers?

People who really suffer on a day-to-day basis all through their lives frequently manufacture their own misery by catastrophizing. Always arriving at the worst possible visualizations of their daily problems, these unfortunates let made up fears control their lives. As parents, wives and friends, they too often impact the lives of those close to them, like the mother in the story. By catastrophizing, a person creates his own distress, which often leads to health problems and premature aging. Catastrophizing most certainly takes the joy out of life and, thwarts one's ability to live fully and happily in Center Court.

Some Risks Are Worth Taking

People who habitually *catastrophize* are never in position to accept challenges. They are not risk takers. They rob themselves of even life's smallest adventures that could add sparkle and success to their lives.

Again I must repeat that fear and *catastrophizing* are not equal. Obviously there are some risks that are worthy of one's fear. For example, if someone told me that walking on a ledge of a building fifty feet high might give me a feeling of uplifting euphoria, I wouldn't be willing to try it. The promise of a thrill wouldn't even tempt me because I'm afraid of suffering physical injury and becoming dependent. I also am absolutely sure that, for me, it's not worth any risk to use drugs or indulge in alcoholic excesses.

But there are, indeed, some risks I take—as long as it's possible to calculate results. If I decide the risk is worth taking a chance, I go for it, For me these are risks that are not liable to result in physical injury or death. If bankruptcy is one of your intrinsic fears, then you will not be an entrepreneur, nor will you make long-shot investments in the stock market.

I suggest you get to know yourself and your threshold of risk taking. Judge your own feelings as to whether or not you want to take any risk in a particular situation. But remember to stay alert for the possibility of beginning to *catastrophize.*

When my son was growing into young manhood, he had an opportunity to make such a choice. Just before summer holidays set in, a major swimming meet was to be held at his school. This moment in his young life would give him a lasting experience and a proud memory that would become valuable to him. He came down with strep throat shortly before the meet, and though he desperately wanted to get out of bed to help his team win, the fever had not yet subsided and the doctor advised that he stay in bed.

However, I realized how much the team and the competition meant to the boy, so I asked the doctor what the possible outcome would be if my son were to swim with a fever and a sore throat, and whether he was contagious. The doctor was shocked at the question from a loving mother. But he indulgently answered me while showing major disapproval. In his judgment if my soon took the prescribed medication but went into the water, he would probably end up spending ten days to two weeks in bed recovering. I asked if it were possible that my son would have to be hospitalized, and the doctor assured me that he would probably not need such extreme treatment.

I left the decision up to him. He weighed the two weeks in bed, and decided to take a chance and compete with his team. The day of the swimming meet was balmy, and I would be there to drive him right home after his race. His buddies were delighted because they had depended on him to slam dunk the win. Indeed, his team got first place. His penalty was the next ten days in bed, just as the doctor had predicted. My son had taken a calculated risk after getting the facts on which to make the decision. For two weeks his friends visited, and my son never complained about those extra days in bed. He had learned how to take a calculated risk and how not to *catastrophize*. He tells me now that this experience had an enormous impact on his decision-making abilities during his entire lifetime; he says he stepped into manhood as a result of that one experience.

ARYNNE SIMON SAYS:

There is no growth without risk.

If you're not sure of what the outcome might be in a particular situation, ask someone with more experience to help you decide which possible outcomes are realistic. You can't always be certain, but you can learn to avoid *catastrophizing*. It's better to look forward with optimism and hope, rather than resist all risk by introducing unwarranted fears. Center Court has a minimum of worry and gloom.

Recognize the Difference

I suggest that when you face an overwhelming problem, you consult the list of real catastrophes; (there is such a list at the end of this chapter). Review the list and ask yourself if your situation fits into one of the real fear categories. If it does, then you've truly got a possible catastrophe to deal with—perhaps a risk not worth taking.

Perhaps you are facing a situation that you would do better not to deal with by yourself. At times when catastrophe threatens, or when there's a death or sudden illness in the family, I suggest you let close friends help you make decisions. When you've got real trouble, delegate your decisions to people you trust, or talk to people who can give you support and advice. Because at a time of real trouble, the emotions tend to work overtime. Remember what you've already learned: when the emotions and the intellect fight, the emotions always win.

But when you're faced with a real catastrophe, live through it; feel the pain, don't deny it. Take care of your body and, after a time, the pain will ease. It's less harmful to your emotions and your body to experience the pain of a real catastrophe than to catastrophize over some imaginary "what-if" scenario.

On the other hand, when you're facing a problem that doesn't fit into one of the categories of a real catastrophe, it is what I call a Golden Problem. (You'll find out more about Golden Problems in a later chapter.) For now, I want you to become vividly aware of the difference between a real catastrophe and catastrophizing.

What to Do?—Be a TV Writer

In order to combat catastrophizing, I would like you to learn to role-play. As soon as you get the first hint of a situation that might trigger catastrophizing, pretend that you're a film or television writer. Imagine that you're writing a story for a horror film or a soap opera. Play it through in you head to the very end and include all the sordid details to see what becomes of your hero or heroine. Do your heroines always wind up dead? Is your hero injured beyond recovery, destined to spend the rest of his life in a wheelchair? Do your lead characters commit suicide or go to prison, or are you the kind of 'writer' who punishes your lead characters by rejections?

In other words, what endings do you make up as the worst possible outcome? If your imaginings belong in fiction or TV drama, you're probably doing the same thing in real life. So play your fears out to their ultimate end to see if you regularly imagine yourself winding up as a homeless person sitting on a park bench with junk in a shopping cart and nowhere to sleep.

You'll soon begin to know your fantasized worst fears, and you'll begin to see them for what they really are. Then, bit by bit, you'll learn to halt your catastrophizing mind.

DEFINITION:

A true catastrophe is:

ANYTHING THAT DRAMATICALLY CHANGES THE COURSE OF YOUR LIFE.

LIST OF CATASTROPHES

- Death of someone close to you
- Your own death
- Physical or emotional illness or injury beyond repair
- Rejection or separation from a loved one (separation that is not permanent, but will be for an extended period of time, may have the same impact as permanent separation)
- Dishonor or acute public embarrassment to yourself or a member of your family
- Bankruptcy
- Loss of political or physical freedom

EMOTIONAL FITNESS EXERCISES

1. Keep the definition of 'catastrophe' clearly in mind. (People tend to view problems as catastrophes. You have a healthy right to feel fear if it is a true catastrophe. But do not transform a problem into a catastrophe.)

2. Make a list of situations where you are likely to *catastrophize.* What are your vulnerable areas?

3. Plot "horror" stories to go with situations that you typically *catastrophize.* Follow them through to their absurd endings.

4. Review regularly to be certain you know the difference between a real catastrophe and catastrophizing.

5. Explain the concept of catastrophizing to at least one other person to anchor firmly in your own mind what you now understand.

6. When you are in a panic or complain of stress, review this chapter. Do what it takes to get yourself back into Center Court. When the fear is real, there are things you can do to cope. Get more information, and discuss the situation with someone who you admire.

   (If you live in Los Angeles, call the counseling firm Talk Works. If you live in another city, seek out a "paid friend"— otherwise known as a psychologist, counselor, or coach— someone who is willing to see you for one session at a time.)

9

A New Way to Test Your IQ

ARYNNE **SIMON SAYS**

Relationships die when manipulations stop working. Either learn to live without manipulative tricks, or find new ones regularly.

Manipulative behavior aggressively pushes people into comers. It's a way of demanding what you want, a control method that negatively pressures others, often without them realizing it. Manipulative behavior is, indeed, aggressive. It leaves the other person feeling vaguely annoyed or taken advantage of—uncomfortable without knowing why. Manipulative behaviors create negative feelings that interfere with healthy, effective functioning between people—whether in the family, at the office, or elsewhere. Eventually, people catch on to the fact that they are being controlled and build up defenses against it.

From groping to salty tears to sultry looks, manipulative behavior renders people helpless because they turn up the intensity of the emotions and push others out of center court. Manipulative behavior prevents people from thinking or working at an optimal level—manipulators must always win the point. It's "their way or the highway."

In this chapter you'll find out how to avoid using manipulative behavior, and what to do when you recognize that someone is trying to control you in this way. Manipulative behavior backs you into the Anger corner, or the Fear corner, or both. There are some people who make you downright uncomfortable, and your feelings are accurate. But you can learn to be aware and in better charge of your responses. Even when people around you are manipulative, you can get into the Center Court of life.

Where Did My Blocks Go?

Children of manipulative parents learn that behavior as they grow up. Later in life, these youngsters become second- or third-generation manipulative adults and are a terror in any relationship.

I had a friend who was a delightful, attractive young woman with everything a young woman might want. On the other hand, nothing was good enough; she demanded all sorts of expensive material possessions, and her spoiled demands and manipulative ways combined to get her most of what she wanted. Her husband was successful, her children were beautiful and bright. And yet this family eventually split apart. Her husband got fed up with her manipulative tactics that included trying to make him jealous. He got tired of his emotions being overworked and decided to leave the relationship.

I remember one day she phoned me, greatly upset after a conference she'd just had with the teacher at the very prestigious private school her children attended. Her son's teacher reported that the six-year-old was doing quite well in schoolwork. But she went on to describe the boy as being destructively manipulative, and recommended that he be taken to see a child psychologist; otherwise, he'd face expulsion. My friend couldn't believe it. How could her son be anything but perfect? He was so intelligent! What could the teacher mean by 'manipulative'?

The teacher had explained by giving my friend an example: when her son was playing blocks with other children, the teacher never witnessed any quarreling or fighting—everything seemed fine. But after observing the youngsters at play, she found that in a little while my friend's son always ended up with all the blocks. The teacher was perceptive enough to wonder how one little boy could always get all of the blocks without causing a fight. This was not a one-time occurrence, the teacher had explained; something like it happened day after day, wherever my friend's son was playing.

I saw what this very perceptive teacher was getting at. She knew from experience that children argue and fight over the possession of toys, or who comes first in a game. As an experienced teacher, she was used to that sort of overt disagreement. If Billy takes Bobby's blocks, Bobby will usually fuss or fight to protect his rights. The fact that one little boy was getting all the toys, cookies, whatever—always without any fighting—indicated that he was putting something over on the other children: he was manipulating them in some way.

My friend didn't want to take her son to the recommended psychologist because it would cost too much and would be a "waste of time." I knew that the school's concerns were valid, and encouraged her to do as they asked. She wanted her son stay at the school, and so to pacify the teacher, she made an appointment with the psychologist.

When she me called the following week, she said with delight, "I want you to know that the psychologist agreed to see us once a week for a month; by the time I finished talking to him, he said he wouldn't charge me anything—not a penny."

Of course you now understand where my friend's son learned how to get everything he wanted. His mother, a master at getting her own way, had been the role model. This bright boy had mastered the art of manipulation at an early age. I always thought the school had done him a great service by pointing it out. I wonder if it made a difference.

I soon got tired of my friend's incessant manipulations and tried to tell her how she exploited people. I was never successful in helping her to perceive manipulative behavior as harmful. She moved away and I never tried to stay in touch with her; frankly I don't miss those afternoon teas in Georgetown when, because of my roller-coaster feelings, I'd eat every cucumber sandwich on the platter.

Her son was a very bright youngster but, like most manipulative people, used his intelligence to assure that he got what he wanted.

Indeed, skilled manipulative behavior requires superior intelligence. As you may know from films like "Matchstick Men" and "Catch Me If You Can," and from books like "The Art of Deception," con men sometimes come with very high IQ scores. It takes an advanced level of smarts to invent the tricks that make their lives easier and satisfies their obsessive need for gratification. And then these smart people assuage their conscience by rationalizing (which is a form of self-manipulation) that they are more entitled to a special life than "ordinary" human beings.

Manipulation Is Natural

Our world respects people who can be independent. We admire people who have made life easier and more comfortable for themselves—people who drive fancy cars, have luxury holidays and big homes. Perhaps you agree with me that we place value on many things and people not worthy of our respect. Wanting the best for oneself is not villainous—it's quite natural and even healthy. So most people occasionally try to manipulate the world to make life better for themselves. Some do it by intimidating others into the corners of Anger and Fear; some use flattery and humor, or other forms of positive manipulation. It's the negative manipulation that I would like to stamp out.

Ultimately, Emotional Fitness requires growing up and finding better ways to handle our own lives, while also taking responsibility for others. Emotional Fitness means knowing how to build and retain strong relationships.

Unfortunately most people have been manipulated into new behaviors by the heavy winds of fear or anger—"Just wait until your daddy gets home." In most cases, we have to learn how to sail our own boats, and even win the race, without storm winds blowing into our sails. Just as the gentle and subtle winds of Mission Bay in San Diego were successfully harnessed by the great sailing champion, Dennis Connor, I encourage you to re-train yourself in order to grow some new muscles for emotional fitness. Develop emotions that will respond to love, fair play, truth, kindness, loyalty, and friendship. You can win the race without being frightened or angry.

Consider actors, models, stand-up comedians and clowns who use positive manipulative behaviors as an intrinsic part of their work to make people laugh, cry, buy, and feel pity. We go to the theatre to be manipulated into moods. Alfred Hitchcock was a master at manipulating viewers into feeling fear as a form of entertainment. The Ralph Lauren ads manipulate us into buying, and for many the act of shopping is also a form of entertainment. And Mr. Rogers manipulated kids into feeling secure and content. All these are positive forms of manipulative behavior, as are singing, cooking, even candles on the dinner table

Over the years, most of my students and clients have admitted that they detest being manipulative or manipulated. Women don't want to have to bat their eyelashes or wear high heels in order to get attention or approval. Men dislike the sound of their angry voices raised in threats in order to get people to respond. In business or at home, people would like to be free of negative manipulative behavior. It erodes the workplace, decreases productivity, becomes self-defeating and breaks up friendships. It's time to want to live your life with simple, straightforward precision.

Typical Manipulative Behaviors

First let's examine some of the typical forms of manipulative behavior that you see around you every day. What games do people play with each other in order to get what they want without asking for it directly? What techniques do they employ?

The Sexy Kind: Some of the easiest ploys to recognize are the batting eyelashes, the smile that can be "heard" on the other end of a phone line, and pathetic crying that many women use to get their way. Playing helpless "weak little me" is also a common manipulative *shtick.* Even the suggestive remarks and groping behaviors of men are not really about sex, but about power.

Expensive Clothing and Make-up: Even if these don't quite fit into the above category, they can be considered a benign form of manipulative behavior. For example, in many sophisticated cities, people choose to wear expensive status-symbol clothing and accessories, and not only for fun and to impress their friends. Clothing is like a protective armor, meant to manipulate the imperious sales personnel, maitre d's and doormen, convincing them that the sta-tus-symbol wearing patron deserves to be treated like a VIP.

Do you realize how many women wear their best clothes just to go shopping? These women (and some men, too) have a desperate need to be noticed and to be treated as VIPs. Advertisers take advan-tage of the marketplace by using manipulative methods to get vul-nerable people to buy their products and, boy, does it work! Our nation has produced two generations, 'baby boomers' and 'gen X'-ers, who would buy anything to lose weight, rather than be rejected or embarrassed because of even five extra pounds in their bathing suits or bikinis. Fear of being rejected is an implied part of any diet program's manipulative marketing.

Even though in most cases the manipulative advertising isn't harmful, how good it is to be wise to Madison Avenue tricks! I sug-gest you stay aware of these forms of negative manipulation. By the time you reach the end of this book, if a maitre d' or a sales clerk can still drive you out of Center Court, I would strongly suggest that you do some deeper digging to find out how your fear and anger are so easily ignited.

Compliments: Another, positive form of social manipulation for getting what you want is the compliment. Most people think that giving a compliment is an admirable, desirable thing to do. And sometimes it is. But other times you praise someone to make him feel good, thinking that when you ask him for what you want, he'll be more likely to give it to you. Soon you'll be able to say what you want first, and then use the compliment as a reward rather than as a bribe. Much more Center Court!

Inappropriate Questions: "Why" is a question that will push someone right back into a corner. A 'why' question is a question that insists on someone giving rationalization and excuses. Watch and see how it puts you on the defensive. There will be more on the 'why' question in Chapter 10, but I mention it here because it's a manipulative trick used by reporters, bosses, children and signifi-cant others. Decide now not to answer a 'why' question. Chapter 10 will give you the thinking behind this suggestion.

Another manipulative technique is the one of asking a question instead of coming out and requesting forthrightly what it is that you'd like. Behind most manipulative questions lurks a fear of saying it straight and possibly getting a 'no'. For example, the question "Where do you want to go to dinner tonight," may really mean "I'd like to get pizza tonight." And "Do you really have to park this far away," might really mean "I'm wearing new shoes and don't want to walk in the rain." Or asking "Are you going to have that information today," instead of simply stating "I'd like to have that report on my desk before 2 o'clock today." (Note: Quality questions are an important aspect of communications, and you'll learn the difference between quality questions and manipulative ones when I take up the subject of assertive communications.)

Whining, Pity, and Martyrdom: Whining, soliciting pity and playing the martyr are other classic manipulative behaviors. Many people seem sweet and innocent, but when they say things like "Isn't it warm in here," rather than "I'd like the window open;" when they say "I can't breathe (hack, hack)—I've got an allergy," instead of "I'd like you to stop smoking," they're communicating manipulatively. A mother will say to her family, "I'm bushed; I've got a splitting headache; I'll never be able to make dinner unless I lie down first," or "My feet are killing me, I've got to sit down," instead of just saying "I want to rest for awhile. I want a little time to myself, and I don't want to be disturbed." She's entitled to that time by herself—but she thinks she has to have an excuse to get it.

From this sort of behavior, children learn that you don't get to do what you want unless you make up a believable reason as subterfuge. This is how parents teach their children that honesty doesn't really work. Believe me, as children we learned all the best tricks of manipulative behavior from our parents.

Imagine an evening when the family has planned to watch a TV show together. A phone call comes in from a friend who wants to come over. As you make a shushing motion to your children, you say into the phone, "Gee, I'd love to have you over tonight, but my husband has a lot of work to do, and I haven't felt too well this afternoon." The children hear you lie and after that, when you lecture them about always telling the truth, it doesn't work. Instead, Center Court communications would have you say, "We've both wanted to get together. Tonight has been planned as a family night. Can we make arrangements for a night next week?" In the first babbling of lies there are twenty-six words. The second, assertive, truthful way has only twenty-two words—direct, fair, and unafraid. Center Court, 100 percent.

Anger, Fear, and Rejection: These are the seriously negative forms of manipulation. Loud voices and threats certainly push people into corners. The sound of anger especially frightens children, and for a limited number of years they respond. But when they figure you out, watch out for these youngsters who will find their own ways to get control away from you.

Scaring people is definitely aggressive: The loving parent who warns, "Don't go outside—you'll catch cold," is using fear to get what he/she wants. Implying an impending catastrophe is how parents manipulate children. A mother says that, if you do something wrong and she finds out about it, she'll punish you. But if she doesn't find out about it, God will know and He will punish you. One way or another, a child had just better do what the parent says.

Playing on a child's fear of being rejected is another negative manipulative device. Children get too much of that from parents and also from their peers. And there's a parallel in the business world. "You'd better do it our way, or we won't pick you for our team, we won't include you in the meetings, you'll get a lousy review, you won't get a promotion...."

Pushing People's Buttons: The surest way to put someone out of control and trap them into over-reactive behavior is to push one of their 'buttons.' If you press someone's button to put them off balance, you may get caught in an explosion. Over my many years of observing manipulative behavior, I've found that all manipulative behaviors backfire.

What are your buttons? Most of us have five or six buttons, and some of them last throughout our lifetime. It's important to know what makes you overreact, what makes you feel that immediate flush at the back of your neck, or the need to fight back. Once you figure out what your buttons are, you are 95 percent of the way towards managing your reactions whenever someone manipulates or pushes one of those buttons. I'll soon give you some effective methods to help you when you feel like exploding, but in most cases I think it's important to accept the reality that you *will* feel the over-reaction when someone hits a button. Going to a therapist so that your buttons will be deactivated is, in my opinion, a waste of money and time. It would be better to know you have some vulnerable areas, and be clear about what they are. Then you can manage your reactions and even stay away from situations that may cause "explosions."

I'm willing to acknowledge some of my own buttons in print. If someone says or implies that I'm not professional or well prepared in my work, or that I don't really work hard enough, I can feel the overreaction begin to bubble up and my emotions start to vibrate. I call that my "You're Not Good Enough" button.

I have a "Your Not a Good Enough Mother/Wife/Daughter/ Sister/Friend" button. When my daughter wanted to go to school in England at the age of thirteen, I thought it would be difficult to be separated from her; (it was). By that time she had been given final say about much of her life, and her judgment was well respected by both her father and me. The experience of a school abroad promised to be a wonderful one for her, and so I struggled to accept an empty nest long before I imagined it would become my reality.

We supported her decision that did, indeed, work out to enrich her life. But to withstand the pain of separation, I set out to work as a consultant—to do my own thing and distract myself from the uncomfortable feeling of missing my baby. And I experienced pain from many well-meaning friends who would say things like, "How could you let her go? I love my children too much to be separated from them." It was implied often, and sometimes even said directly, that something was lacking in my feelings as a mother if I could let my daughter leave home for a school so far away. I suffered many emotional explosions because my "Not Good Enough Mother" button was regularly being pushed.

Eventually I learned to handle these encounters from Center Court. When asked about her life in England, I was prepared to say, "Her being away has been difficult time for me, but I believe that to love something is to set it free. Would you like to know more about her life in England?" In other words, I knew that I could get hurt if I was not ready to protect myself. This is one way to shield your buttons from being pushed without building high walls or blaming others.

Then there's my "Ethical" button. Just imply that I am not honest, loyal, truthful or the like, and this button starts pounding. Do you have one of these ethical buttons? Okay then, start your button list with "You Are Not Ethical." It's the first one on your list; you need to identify at least four more.

I have a "Vanity" button. Yes, even at my advanced age! If I'm not at least as well put together as others my age, I still have something of a problem in a social setting.

Are you vain and eager for compliments? If anyone says, "Well—you've put on a few pounds since we last met," and you feel like exploding, add the word 'Vanity' as the second entry on your list. (These days, age jokes also offend me and I have added 'Age' to my list.)

I also have a button that says, "You're Just a Woman." Oh, boy, does that one get to me!

Some people overreact if someone pushes a button by lashing out physically (think Mike Tyson or OJ Simpson). But I overreact by over-talking. So if you push one of my buttons and catch me off guard, get ready for a lecture. If you tend to overreact in non-acceptable ways—hitting, stealing, drinking, driving too fast or spending money you don't have—I suggest you make a clear list of what causes you to explode. Review this list very often; daily, if necessary. In every situation, often without meaning to, people lean against your buttons and voila —you are in big trouble!

I often teach over-reactive behavior by giving an extreme description of a button-pressing fight. Consider a long–married couple, each of whom knows the other's buttons all too well. On the way home from a party, the wife says, "You acted like a young jock tonight. You were ogling the girls and you embarrassed me. Other people were looking at you like, 'Who does that old man think he is!'—with your big belly and how bald you're getting."

She's hitting his 'Getting Old' button, with the bald spot thrown in. So he strikes back with, "You could lose a few pounds, too. Thin turns me on—not your fat ass."

She counters with, "Who has to please you—your don't even have the money to send me to a spa (Now his "Success" button has been punched). I heard you show off about your new job—big deal! ('You are a phony!') And you bragging that you gave Roger the money you owed him and he never even counted it—I'll bet you cheated him! My father would never have cheated a friend ('So you're dishonest, too, and not as good as my dad!'). Why don't you go back to your mommy and grow up? And as for your sex appeal—you weren't the first guy for me; and frankly, you're not a great lover."

She has hit every possible button her husband could have, and you know as well as I do that she's bound to get all *her* buttons pounded before she gets home. This couple is in for a terrible weekend.

An exaggeration? Not really? Look at the divorce rate.

ARYNNE **SIMON SAYS:**

To know each other well is to know each other's buttons. To love each other well is to know the buttons, but never press them.

As a matter of fact, many people are unwilling to establish close relationships because when they know each other very well, they know each other's buttons and can use them to inflict pain. The hurt of getting our buttons pounded can be severe, so we suppress our desire for a meaningful, close relationship and hope that we're safe from anyone pressing our buttons. This fear of a close relationship robs people of the joy of getting close enough to let down barriers. Look for the kind of powerful relationship where two people know each other very well and protect each other from hurt.

And how does button-pressing factor into the work environment? You've just been asked for an opinion and have given it. Then your boss turns to your rival and asks, "Tom, do you see it that way, too?" It's a fair question, but it feels as if your boss is announcing, "Your opinion isn't quite good enough." Oops, there's that "Not Good Enough" button.

By now I've learned to spot a button-pusher coming at me, and so I've put up some verbal guards. So I might respond, "You've just hit a sensitive spot with me. Are you really saying that all men are better drivers than women?" In the chapter on Listening Skills, you'll learn how to use quality questions to help slow down your emotional explosions.

Perhaps you will take away from this chapter a new understanding of button pressing. You can stay in Center Court even when someone is playing an unfair game—but you must be prepared by having identified your weak spots well in advance of a situation. If your over-reactions are too deep and too many, or can only be quieted by alcohol, drugs, hitting, stealing, spending, speeding, eating or sexual acts, you will need to find out more about your over-reactive behavior. A therapist (or as I call them, a "paid friend") can help you investigate the source for your overreactions, as well as a solution. But for most of us, it's just important to stay aware of what causes us to overreact, and to be prepared for handling these moments by using the verbal skills suggested in this book.

Arynne SIMON SAYS:

Manipulating people is the opposite of building relationships.

And don't forget our earlier discussion; how some forms of manipulative behavior are quite positive—and not just the ones used by entertainment professionals. These are fun and don't involve the corners of Anger or Fear. Things like clothes that are a little sexy in a social situation encourage flirting; not a bad thing. Jokes, lyrics, even fake jewels or art can change your mood and lift your spirit. So I apply the word 'manipulative' to the destructive, undermining sort of behavior that pushes people into anger and fear, or the combination of those, which you know by now cause dysfunctional anxiety.

There is a Time Limit on Manipulative Behavior

Manipulative behavior can lose its effectiveness. People, even children, catch on to the drill, and they cease to react. A mother's shouting loses its impact after a while; the hypochondriac's complaints are ignored. Even tears won't get a reaction. People who are manipulated grow thick skins to protect their feelings from being manipulated.

By the time we've grown up, we've each latched on to a favorite manipulative style. We may have learned it from a parent or a sibling, or invented it for ourselves: the whiny voice, the angry voice, the sighs, the sulk, the sarcasm or the manipulative questions, or some of the many others. For a while, these work and we get what we want. But beware. Over time, what works today will not get even a flicker of response farther down the road. So what do most folks do? They escalate the level of their habitual manipulative behavior and the intensity of their anger. But to work, even threats will need to become more ominous. The sulks will have to last longer and, when they no longer work, it may be necessary to quit a job or a relationship and start over with new people. A child runs away, a husband or wife asks for a divorce; one way or another, when the manipulations cease to work, the relationship is over. New subjects are needed for old manipulations to be effective. So many people live on these manipulative merry-go-rounds.

You Can Do It All Without Manipulation

But the fact is that you can get the life you want, and even the attention you need, without manipulating others. You can even close sales without manipulation, and you can get others to listen to you, give you service, respect your rights, respect your wishes—all without manipulative behavior, without deception, without aggression, without straining relationships to the breaking point.

An Example of How to Get What You Want Effectively

The following is an example of an altogether harmless manipulation, but I offer it as a step in showing you that you can live life without any manipulation. Then I will allow you to put the non-destructive manipulations back, if you want to.

Here's a simple situation, an everyday version of something that many sales reps do quite often. You walk into a bakery to buy some chocolate-chip cookies, and there at the front of the tray are four crispy brown ones—just the way you prefer them. Those are the four you want, but you know that the clerk is not going to be too thrilled about letting you choose which ones you get. So you begin by saying, "Oh, you've remodeled the shop; it looks better in here with the counter a bit lower. I think the tables in the back are great and next time I will have a cup of coffee. Much better…good idea." After you've paved the way with compliments, then you say, "Those four brown-edged cookies in the front—those are the ones I want. Would you do me a favor and let me have those four?"

Do you spot the manipulative stuff? Not awful but, in my opinion, not necessary. How about replaying this scenario without the manipulative compliments? Just walk in, decide what you want and say pleasantly, "I'd like the four brown-edged cookies in the front, please." Maybe the clerk will reach for them, but if not, say, "Okay, rules are rules. Pick out the four crispiest ones you can." When you've got the cookies in the bag, then take the time to say, "I really like the remodel and the fact that I can get a cup of coffee."

Try to put the compliments at the end of a transaction. This is just a dry run to see how much manipulation you can take out of your life and still make it through. If you take the time to say kind things to the sales person, even if you don't get what you want, you'll know you're in Center Court—100 percent. Remember the feeling, because that's the extent of effort you need to put into a transaction like buying cookies. If you *have* to get the four cookies you want, or the table you want in a restaurant, that is tantrum behavior—not assertive behavior. Let's get your life into perspective.

Do Your Business First

Following the cookie example, I believe it's effective in business to save your compliments for the end of a transaction. Practice first on friends and family. If you call a friend to postpone a luncheon date, try: "I'd like to change our luncheon day. Next Thursday turns out not to be a good time for me." Only after you've managed some new arrangements (but maybe gotten a little flack in the process), then get into the personal stuff: "By the way, how are you? And how are the children? Did you have a fun vacation?"

For a while put the personal talk at the end of your conversations. It's best to end on an up-beat note, and a better way to reinforce relationships. Use kind words to reward instead of to bribe.

Please remember, most manipulative behavior is not a high crime. Understand that you may have never learned other ways to make life comfortable for yourself. When someone tries to manipulate you, don't get angry or put them down. They're just doing the best they can. Stay aware of how much of life is played manipulatively, and deal with it directly. This kind of Center Court behavior feels so good! Give it a try.

EMOTIONAL FITNESS EXERCISES
TO IMPROVE MANIPULATIVE MUSCLES

1. Make a list of the manipulative behavior you see being used around you—spouse, children, friends, boss, fellow workers.

2. Make a list of the manipulative behaviors you use most often on other people.

3. Complete your list of your buttons and make copies of this list to carry with you or post over your desk.

4. Decide how you overreact, and be honest about it. Do you eat too much? Talk too much? Hit? Get angry? Flirt? Or do you get sarcastic or sulk? Do you cry? Threaten?

5. Prepare a few statements you are comfortable making when someone hits one of your buttons. Practice these and get ready with them.

10

Three Boxes of Effective Speech

ARYNNE **SIMON SAYS**

Words are either tools for building relationships, or weapons for revenge.

B y now, you've become aware of what it means to play in Center Court without Anger or Fear, and you've learned how to hear what people are really saying without being manipulated. You know how to recognize behavior in others that might push you out of Center Court, and perhaps you've even built up some muscle tone about saying clearly what you want. And I hope you're beginning to know what you want, and building muscles to help you have the strength and courage to request what you'd like. What I want most of all is for you to remember that a 'good day' is a day when you know what you want and have the courage to just say it.

As a matter of fact, you've been practicing a bit of assertive language skills while you did your 'no' muscle exercises.

Language is the most powerful tool we use to share ideas and to network knowledge so that civilization can grow. Language can also be used for building relationships, although we recognize that not all relationships are built or broken on words alone. But in our social structure, we understand how words can be used either as tools for building relationship or weapons of destruction. For example, I've warned that the word 'why' is the handgun of communications, killing relationships; it's typically used to trap someone or get revenge.

Arynne SIMON SAYS:

Neither use nor answer a 'why' question.

I've taught this concept often enough to know that some of you will immediately think that I'm dead wrong—that 'why' is an effective word in getting you information that you need. Please be patient, for I have every intention of expanding on this observation. You may soon come to agree that there are many better ways of phrasing a question for gathering even hard facts and information without needlessly putting pressure on others. There is no surer way to drive someone into the back corners of life, and out of Center Court, than the word 'why.'

Our objective is to communicate in a way that improves both information gathering and relationship building. One without the other is failed communication. A meeting that is overflowing with ideas but injures the feelings and hurts a team's cohesiveness is a wasted meeting, no matter how valuable the ideas. A meeting is where people exchange information *and* build relationships. So in business, I suggest that you measure the effectiveness of your meetings by the way the team members listen and learn from each other, as well as from the innovative ideas.

At one of the major Silicon Valley companies, the executive team would come out of their meetings sweating, with many of the men showing the intense, angry red of a flush on the back of their necks. A few of them would march away from the conference room in agitated frustration, and I could hear the distant slamming of heavy doors. The candy wrappers were scattered all over the conference table. The room had clearly been the setting for volatile interchanges. Yet the CEO would often come out saying, "Great Meeting."

As a consultant, I knew that these meetings shattered the team and were the cause of some of these talented people laying plans to leave. That CEO was judging his meetings on sound decibels, and he promoted the most fractious fighters on the team. His companies, this one and the ones he later was chosen to lead, all failed. His meetings were too costly for the companies in many important ways; his marriage eventually suffered a divorce. Smart man—but with no understanding of what real communication is meant to accomplish.

"Help, I Need a Ride."

Imagine yourself in the following situation: It's the end of a busy working day. You're a little tired and eager to get home, when another employee rushes up to your desk, obviously distressed, and says, "I need a favor—the repair shop just called and said my car is not worth fixing and my best friend can't give me a ride home from work any more. You live in my area, so would you please give me a ride home after work?"

Admittedly, this is a problem you understand, and your co-worker is appealing to you to help solve it. You're a kind and fair person, but you sure don't want the responsibility of driving someone home after work; you look forward to a chance of being alone in your car. And it sounds like a situation that could repeat itself every night, at least for a while. So what do you say?

What would an aggressive person say? A convenient lie typically comes to mind, like, "I don't go home after work—I usually meet some friends for a drink." Or it's possible that the aggressive person might overreact and say, "No way. Why ask me? We hardly know each other." Or a manipulative response could be, "Oh, gee, I'd love to take you, but I've had problems with my insurance company, and I'm afraid to drive somebody on a regular basis."

At the other extreme, a passive person might say, "Okay, no problem." But then after thinking it over, the passive person feels taken advantage of and wishes he'd finished the book on assertive behavior. He falls asleep that night plotting a way to get out of the promise, maybe by saying something like, "I'd love to be able to help you out but my wife wouldn't let me."

Using Your Brain

In situations like this one, a lot of people feel trapped. They're angry or frightened, and they respond intuitively, saying the first thing that comes to mind. But since they are out of balance, their brains are not functioning—their emotions take control. You already know that when the emotions and the brain fight, the emotions always win.

And you've already learned that emotions never help when problem solving. So you're going to slow down, eliminate the anxiety and get back in Center Court, where your active brain can help you follow through on what's best for you. For a while, just like when you learn a new tennis serve or golf stroke, you must think it through. It will seem like you're living in slow motion. But after enough practice shots, your reactions will speed up and it will become integrated into your life. You were willing to do that when you learned to use the Internet, serve a tennis ball, shoot a basket, dance or play the piano. Now is your chance to slow down and learn to live a better life by using more accurate communications. And it will only slow you down for a short while.

What you say must be a complete communication: get your ideas across and also protect the relationship. With that as a measure for your success, you can learn to respond appropriately to the person who 'needs' a ride. As we go through this and several other fictional problems step by step, you'll be rehearsing for future, real-life assertive problem solving.

Help Her Help Herself

Is the person who needs a ride frightened? Yes. And probably angry, too, to be faced with this dilemma that has by now become a full-blown anxiety. It will be better if she finds her own solution to the problem, but at this moment she can't seem to come up with any plan—except to count on you. But when people find their own best solutions to problems, they feel much better for having done so. If you truly respect people, you depend on their ability to help them help themselves. And they will.

So you can agree to think about this situation and promise a decision tomorrow at lunchtime. Probably by then the situation and the solution will have changed. I learned this way of handling decisions from former President and five-star general Dwight Eisenhower, who once explained that the words 'I'll think about it' are much more powerful than either 'yes' or 'no.'

The Three Boxes of Effective Speech

But there's a better way to design your verbal responses: by using the Three Boxes of Effective Speech. These three boxes show the order and content of assertive speech. I suggest you use it as a road map for all communications—both spoken and written. It doesn't work for a news story or a PR release, but it works for everything else. So memorize it, and follow it step by step to deal with whatever problem you face—whether it's a presentation, a speech, a book report or just saying 'no.'

The Three Box Method is summarized in Fig. 10-1.

BOXES & THEIR FUNCTIONS
ACTION CHOICES

BOX 1—Make the audience connection

- Describe the situation.
- Describe how you think the other person or group views the situation or problem.
- Use stories, allegories, anecdotes that engage the audience's brain. (Jokes, if used at all, must be very carefully selected.)
- If the subject is a difficult one, ask for permission or give warning.

BOX 2—Present your case

- State the facts (the number of facts used will vary with the situation and person/people involved).
- Describe your experience with similar situations.
- Relate an anecdote or use an allegory that may further explain a fact.
- Remember to state facts, not feelings.
- Optional: May include objections or resistance if you're not doing Q and A.

BOX 3—State what you want

(This is the action statement, or closing the sale, or a chance to show your leadership.)

- State clearly and simply what you'd like; request, suggest, or tell the audience to consider or do; be specific, so others have a chance to succeed for you.
- In difficult situations, involve the other person or members of the team in the solution.
- Be sure the action items are clearly stated.

IMPORTANT: Think ahead and know Box 3—your request or action statement—*before you begin.* Speak from Box 1 to Box 2 to Box 3—not back and forth between boxes.

Figure 10-1. **The Three Box Method for Effective Communications**

What You Want Goes Last

In the sample situation about giving someone a ride home, what you want goes into the last box. Ask yourself what would mean the most to you at the end of your workday. Do you want a companion to talk to on the drive home? Or do you want the privacy of being by yourself and a chance to sort out the day's events while listening to your favorite DJ? To stay in Center Court, you must always know what you want, like, prefer or demand. It all starts with this.

ARYNNE SIMON SAYS:

Whenever you are upset or stressed or feeling trapped, you must search for what you really want. Just knowing what you want will quiet things down enough for you to make a plan.

So in Box 3, you'll state what you want. It comes last, but get the statement ready as a first step. All effective communication begins by planning the bottom line. Handling any situation from Center Court starts with asking yourself, "What do I want?"

Hopefully you've been doing the Wanting exercises, so that what you want in this situation will come quickly to your mind—not what you 'need' or what you 'have to have.' Remember, if you have to *get* everything you want, you're living in the middle of a tantrum. You merely have to *know* what you want and be able to express it.

The ride-home request has pushed you out of Center Court if you feel yourself getting angry – "How dare she ask me for a ride?!?" Or frightened – "Gee, if I don't give her a ride, she'll talk against me to my boss." To get back into Center Court quickly, decide what it is that you want and put it mentally into Box 3. But don't say it now!

If It's First, It Gets Lost

Many people communicate incorrectly. Do not begin by blurting out what you want, and follow it up with a list of excuses or reasons to support your preference.

When a customer returns something to a store, they say, "I want my money back." And then they say, "I bought this here a week ago, and it didn't wash well, and I've been a customer here for ten years, and I don't see how this could have cost so much when it didn't even hold up in the wash." The bewildered clerk says, "And what is it you want?" The statement of what she wanted got buried under the excuses that followed. So you will always *end* your communications on what you would like to see done.

So first decide what you want for yourself—but say it last. This technique is also valuable when writing business letters or making presentations or short speeches. You can manage to do this without even writing anything down if you follow the procedure mapped out in the communications road map. It's easy, fast and it always works. This system guarantees that you will have a workable structure and will not be over-talking any issue or answering a question by talking all around it.

Box 1

Box 1 has several different functions, as you can see from the chart. After deciding on what you want, your next step is to consider what to say in Box 1 that will protect or build a relationship. This can be done by restating or describing the situation, or by expressing a common concern. If you're talking to someone close to you, Box 1 can contain a statement that reveals your understanding and feelings. In the case of someone you work with or don't know very well, it's best to avoid expressing your feelings.

So in the situation we're practicing on, you might decide to say, "Without a car to depend on, life gets really stressful." Or, "These days everyone depends on their cars." If you're talking to someone you know very well, you might prefer to say, "I understand how upsetting it will be for you without a car." In Box 1, you appropriately restate the problem to let the other person know that you're listening, that you've heard them and (if it's appropriate) that you care.

The emotionally fit individual knows what he wants, but he wants to acknowledge the other person as being valuable, too. Box 1 recognizes the value of the other person and shows him that you respect him as a fellow human being. As I've already said, and want to re-emphasize: Box 1 builds relationships. It's very difficult to slow down enough to include this first statement. I know when you're handling a difficult situation, you're eager to get to the facts and conclusion, but I suggest you slow down.

Box 2

Believe it or not, despite the fact that Box 2 will communicate information, it is the least important of all three statements. Box 2 is the one most people use, overrate, and abuse.

The second statement is when you offer a fact—not an excuse, but a true and honest fact if you have one to include. Use only one, and say it only once. Many people think they have to give a long list of facts, and they come off sounding like children.

Just remember that a fact is not a reason. What seems perfectly reasonable to you is never reasonable to somebody else when they want something. So stick to the facts. You can give a child, a friend or a direct report twenty reasons why you can't do something, but if they want it very badly at that moment, your reasons won't make a bit of sense to them.

Box 1, Box 2, Box 3

To that person who's in a state of distress over not having a car to drive home in, you could say:

- Box 1: These days everyone depends on their cars.
- Box 2: It's a real problem to be without transportation.
- Box 3: I really want some privacy at the end of the day.

Is this person going to respond positively to these three sentences? Absolutely not. Anything except hearing a clear and enthusiastic, "I'd be glad to be your driver" will not be acceptable. In fact, you'll probably get back something close to: "How could you do this to me? Everyone said you were nice. But I don't think you're nice at all." A woman might even try a few tears or a wobbly chin. But you're already familiar with manipulative methods some people might use to try getting what they want. If this happens, you go through Box 1, 2, and 3 again, but with slightly different words. For example:

- Box 1: When things go wrong, they really hit all at once.
- Box 2: This will be tough to figure out.
- Box 3: I want to preserve my time alone in the car at the end of the day.

You may have to repeat this process several times, until the person gets it or stomps away. Just a few pages ahead, I'll explain yet another way to move distress from heart to head. After all, it's in the head that all problems get solved, where people have a chance to calm themselves down and solve their own dilemmas.

The object through this interchange is to try to retain ownership of Center Court, doing it in a straight and honest way that doesn't push others into a state of greater anxiety. When dealing with people close to you, this assertive process is all the more important. With family members and close friends, express understanding of their feelings before you give a fact and say what you want for yourself.

Once again, the most difficult part of this new communication skill is to start speaking in Box #1. Most people jump into Box 2 or 3 right off. If you find you're having this problem, think of a tennis coach teaching you how to serve. The way the ball is thrown into the air is as important, or maybe more so, than the power of your service stroke. Don't give up. Throw the ball up accurately. Speak in Box 1. It will all come together sooner than you think. The direct simplicity of the Three Box road map of communications will help you to think a situation through; what you say and how you say it is the game of communications and, therefore, of relationships.

Practice Using the Three Boxes

You may want to keep a copy of the Three Box road map on your desk, or draw it into your PDA. When the phone rings or when you go to a meeting, look at the boxes and reply by following the format. For example: "These days people are having trouble paying bills on time. The fact is that it's hard to run a business when cash flow is slow. I'll be waiting until the 15th to pay the bill." Follow the road map accurately: Box 1, Box 2, Box 3. And do not give in to the tendency to over-talk the situation.

Another example: "No one likes getting up in the morning. I have an important business meeting first thing. I'd like us to finish breakfast and be ready to start the day in half an hour."

And another one: "I understand how important it is for you to have a new dress for the party. Dad and I decided to go easy on the expenses until we catch up. I'd like us to work tonight on assembling an outfit out of things you own that could look brand new to your friends but doesn't cost us anything extra this month."

At first it may be difficult to create the words to fit the boxes, but when you've actually done it a few times, you'll be surprised at how easy it gets. A great way to practice is by answering your emails this way. When you're doing the Three Boxes in writing, you don't just have to think about Box 3—you can actually begin by writing your Box 3 statement. Then you'll scroll up and write Box 1 and then Box 2.

As you practice using the Three Box technique, it will become very natural—a part of you. In order to give you a better sense of how the boxes will work for you, I'll share a few more examples of situations and how students handled them.

Give That Man a Rose

The first week after learning about the Three Boxes, a corporate student of mine had a rewarding experience. She had been upset with neighbor who had several cars in the family; the father always parked his huge Humvee in front of her house. She hadn't known how to handle the situation without the chance of causing bad feelings. When she learned about the Boxes, she planned what she was going to say to him, but knew she needed a day when she had some extra courage.

One evening she went out to water her rose garden at a time she knew he would be coming home. They said their pleasant "hellos" and then, as she afterward described it to the class, she jumped into Box 1: "These days people have a lot of cars and big ones are the best."

He replied, "Yup, my Humvee is my pride and joy."

She was ready for Box 2. "I love looking at the mountains, but with a large car parked in front, I can't enjoy the view." Then she rushed right into Box 3 with, "I wish that bit of space in front of my windows could be left open."

He shrugged and said, "Sure."

So she cut off a rose and handed it to him. And he kept his word—it was as simple as that. She told us she was sure that, had she made a big deal about it instead of just saying what she wanted, he would have given her a headache. This irritation had bothered her for months. She had been nervous about trying the new assertive language, but luckily the results were immediate and easy. She reported to the class that the secret was in knowing how to say what she really wanted.

Sample Situations

Students in my classes have worked on several difficult situations with success. Let's see how they've handled a few. We'll consider a situation that involves turning down a friend's request to accompany him to a movie when you want to stay home and catch up on paper work. Or telling a host at a party that you want to leave early. Or telling a friend that, since she's late for your appointment to help her with a speech, you have run out of time for working with her.

I Want to Stay Home Tonight

In the first example, you've decided that you want to stay home and do some catch-up work. But a friend from work calls and wants the two of you to go to a movie. You'd been looking forward to staying home to do nothing but read and catch up. You had even written it into your schedule with an exclamation mark next to this note, meaning "At last and definitely!"

It's important for you to be able to organize your own time and not be made to feel you're letting a friend down just because you want to stay home for an evening. The friend says, "Come on, it got great reviews. And I'll even do the driving. I'll pick you up in a half hour."

Your reply could go like this: Box 1, "Everyone's been saying that this is one great caper film." Box 2, "I was looking forward to staying home tonight." Box 3, "I'd like to schedule the movie for another night."

The friend will surely whine and say "c'mon."

So you go back to Box 1, "You really want to go to the film tonight." Box 2, "I appreciate your giving me a chance to go with you." Box 3, "I definitely want to stay home tonight, and hope we can do it another time."

Just keep a sense of yourself and what it is you want. Then if the friend is still annoyed, you may want to say something like: "I really appreciate that you called, and I hope we can set something up for next week or so." Then just let it go. People get over their disappointment, and whatever hard feelings they may have as a result, on their own. Believe me, it won't last for very long.

I Want to Go Home Now

The next problem concerns telling the host at a party that you're tired and you want to go home, even though it's early in the evening and he had hoped his guests would all stay late. I suggest you expect some pressure from your host, since being the first guest to leave may give others the idea that the party's over.

Your host says, "What gives? Why is your coat on?"

And you say something like: Box 1, "You've worked so hard on this shindig and, by the look on your face, you're disappointed that I'm about to leave." Box 2, "I'm really tired, I almost decided not to come." Box 3, "By going home now, I can catch up on the sleep I've been missing."

The host is hurt: "I thought I could count on you to help make this party a success."

Box 1 again: "I'm flattered that you counted on me and I understand your disappointment." Box 2, "I can hardly stay awake." Box 3, "I want to go early, but first I'll tell everyone not to follow my example."

This incident is not a catastrophe, although it may feel like one to your host. If the party-giver puts undue pressure on you, he's being manipulative. He's thinking that his party will be a failure, and even though he's a friend, he is pressuring you out of Center Court. He may be angry at you, figuring that as a friend you *shouldn't* be the first to leave. And he's afraid people will see you go and decide you thought the party was a bore. But you don't have to react to his fear and anger. You can stay in charge of your own behavior and do what's best for you. You did, after all, come to the party, and you do understand his disappointment. Disappointment is *not* a catastrophe.

I Want to Keep My Schedule

You've promised to spend an hour helping a client who has to make a presentation to her executive committee. She's due to come to your apartment at 10, leaving you plenty of time to get to your 11:30 appointment. You told her you would do her a favor and squeeze her in, but she doesn't arrive until 10:45—leaving you only ten minutes to work with her before you have to leave. She comes in nervous and out of breath and apologizes. She expects a full hour with you because she's worried about her presentation and won't accept that you'll actually "abandon" her. She says, "I can't wait to get started on this presentation and I need your input and help. You're the best! No wonder our company uses you so often."

Box 1, "You're really in a panic over this presentation and want my help." Box 2, "It's forty-five minutes into the time I set aside to help you." Box 3, "I'll work with you for ten minutes, and then I want to get ready to leave for my next appointment—the one I told you about."

She's distraught: "You promised to help me. I can't believe you'd do this to me."

You respond: Box 1, "These presentations are very important to people's careers. I understand that." Box 2, "Ten minutes is as much as I can give you right now." Box 3, "I want to be on time for my next appointment."

She's beside herself with anger and fear: "I've talked to some of the others about you. They said you'd let me down! Wait until this gets around the department."

Box 1, "I can see that you're really worried about this presentation." Box 2, "I'd like to use these last minutes to help you get started." Box 3, "Please assure me that for our next appointment you'll be on time."

This client does have a problem, but it is not a catastrophe. There is no way you can reassure her, since she's so upset and has even tried to manipulate you with a threat that you will lose the company account. You kept your part of the bargain. I advise that you stick with your decision, remembering that you have your own career to consider. She'll soon realize that you did nothing wrong, and get over this incident. There is no reason for you overreact to her insensitive behavior. Let it go. Meanwhile, don't let this behavior get you anxious and drive you out of Center Court; you have your own work to do.

Let People Know

If people are usually late coming to dinner, and it bothers you, say something to them about it. If you don't, you may spoil your own evening every time they are invited.

Box 1, "Especially with our traffic the way it is these days, it's often hard to be on time." Box 2, "I plan to serve dinner at 8:30." Box 3, "I'd like it if dinner could be on time."

You don't have a right to be angry if you don't get what you want; you do have the right to request that others respect your schedule. Say what you'd like and you'll feel better. And then there's a better chance that your guests will show up on time. Set up your guests, your significant others, your children and your employees to succeed for you. Request what you'd like; more often than not, you may be pleasantly surprised.

Rely on the Words

When you use the Three Boxes, don't join them together with 'and,' 'but,' 'however,' 'because,' or any other words that imply a logical order. Human behavior is often not a logical process; the words you speak will be more clearly heard when they stand by themselves. The connection between the boxes will not hold up the way a philosophical syllogism does. You may think that Box 1 plus Box 2 result in Box 3. They do not.

When someone thinks they need something, nothing you say really makes any emotional sense to them. What they need you to do is agree with them and say yes to them. But the best thing you can do is to be forthright and truthful in your speech. Make three specific statements. Have confidence in the words. Don't manipulate others into agreeing with you by dramatizing with your voice, shoulders, eyebrows, etc. It's much easier for people to hear what you say when they're not distracted by your movements. Don't frighten people or take away their freedom to disagree with you.

The result of this kind of direct, honest speech is that it makes you someone who is comfortable to deal with and far easier to relate to. People will think your interpersonal skills have been amazingly improved, without knowing exactly how you've changed or what you're doing. I offer the Three Box road map as a way to transform your delivery of your wants and ideas into communications of quality and effectiveness.

The Complete Listener

In your lifetime, you can't have missed the message that it's important to be a good listener. That message is frequently aimed at people in sales and told to business people as a way to become liked by others in order to increase sales. What a crass reason for listening at a quality level.

It would be better if we could all find better ways to establish relationships that work. If you're a manager or leader, you are attempting to build teams and businesses. If you are a community leader, you're attempting to establish new ways that can make life better for everyone. If you're a parent, you are trying to raise children who can solve problems and establish a new and higher level of civilization. We must all listen to each other and hear each other.

Perhaps you've read a book or taken a course to improve your listening skills. I've met people who have taken one of the typical listening courses, and am appalled by a simplistic technique being widely taught that I call "the echo system." You know—the one where you're trained to feed back the words that have just been spoken. This outdated method makes people—especially children— quite angry. The echo method usually sounds like, "In other words what you're telling me is that _____." It's a condescending communication tool and is not okay—not even in an auditorium during a question and answer session. There are better, more interesting, less offensive ways to let people know you were attentive and that you did, indeed, listen and hear.

Listening the New Way—the Simon Way

Learning to listen and being perceived as a listener are both important. Listening to get the facts, information and knowledge is definitely a vital tool for people who live and work together. Listening as a way to polish relationships is also absolutely essential.

So the measurement of successful listening has two parts to be rated. Listening to capture the message is only one part of the totality of being an effective listener. The other part is listening that includes a new awareness of the need to be perceived as a good listener. People need to be listened to, and will appreciate your skills as a listener only if they receive cues that you are hearing them.

It's a given fact that smart people understand what's being said much faster than others. Very savvy people have a way of picking up a fact, idea, or piece of information as soon as it's out of someone's mouth. These people (you may be one of them) impressed their teachers in class by always raising their hands before others.

But, beware. I have found that the smarter you are, the less likely it is that you are a quality listener. You may think you're a good listener because you pick up information at top speed. But you are *not* a complete listener if you are not *perceived* as a listener. Missing this second part of the listening equation can prevent you from being an effective spouse, manager, parent, or entrepreneur. If you are an incomplete listener, you can easily parrot back what has just been said. You can get good grades on tests but somehow other people feel as though they haven't been listened to.

It's not unusual for a father or mother to tell me with great assurance, "Of course I listen to my son. I know his girlfriend's name and I know what kind of car he wants next summer. I know that he has some worries about getting on the first team and that he'd like to go to an Eastern college. Of course I listen to my son."

Yet the son says, "My father never heard a word I said in my whole life." Yes, when it comes to listening, perception is reality. If the son, the direct report, the significant other, doesn't feel engaged and validated, the listening process has failed.

You can easily become a quality listener, a complete listener, and it doesn't involve gripping the end of a desk and telling yourself, "Listen, listen; don't talk—just listen."

ARYNNE **SIMON SAYS:**

Letting someone talk without interrupting them doesn't give you the title of a "quality listener."

How Can You be Perceived as a Quality Listener?

Becoming a quality listener involves these principles:

1. The head plus the heart equals complete listening.
2. Giving and receiving information involves the head.
3. Then you need to give the speaker the *feeling* of being heard.

Only when a feeling of being heard is combined with the ideas being transferred, can the perception of being listened to be complete. Then you can be considered a "Complete and Quality Listener."

The feeling of being heard comes only when you give someone the opportunity to answer quality questions. As long as you speak in the affirmative—with sentences that have a period or an exclamation mark at the end—even when you speak to acknowledge what has just been said, you will not be perceived as a quality listener. People only feel listened to when they are asked and can respond to quality questions.

In communication, the quality question is the best of tools. As you dig for information with quality questions, the speaker will know that you are listening and hearing, and will feel acknowledged knowing that you want more of his/her thinking.

Without quality questions as part of your speech pattern, people know that you are listening at a superficial level. Unless you learn how to ask quality questions, you cannot be perceived as a strong or effective listener. And, as a quality listener, you'll be surprised and delighted at the new shadings and dimensions that will be added to what you thought were easy-to-grasp facts or ideas.

At a meeting, for example: when the conversation turns to team building that includes a plan for an upcoming offsite, someone says, "Let's have three half-day offsites, so we don't get so far behind in our work." The smart people in the room get this idea very fast. No one asks for any additional information, and this first idea is quickly buried under the next idea from some very fast and smart member of the team. The manager of this group has long been saying that he/she wants to encourage building a collaborative team with cohesiveness and mutual respect. Allowing any idea to be buried under another idea is equivalent to the original idea being dismissed.

Let's back up a minute to see how quality listening can improve this meeting by acknowledging each individual, and how a company that says people's ideas are their number one asset can make that statement come alive.

It's up to the manager or facilitator to say to the second speaker:

Manager: "Just a minute, Howard—let's explore Chris's idea. Chris, are you suggesting that we hold breakfast meetings for three or four days in a row, rather than shut down for three days?"

Chris: "Something like that. I've heard a number of people in the group say that it's too frustrating to come back to four days of piled-up work. Meeting at the Jay Hotel at about 8 and staying through lunch would still give us four hours back at our desks. I think it would be less of a wipe out."

Manager: "Have you done this before somewhere else, and did it work? Hold on a minute Howard—we'll get to your idea next. Let's give Chris a chance."

Chris: "Not quite the way we're planning, but I've heard that it worked over in the Tech Support Group and I'd be glad to find out more about that."

Manager: "Let's get that information. Now, Howard—you seem eager to get your idea on the table. What would you like to suggest?"

And then after Howard speaks, the manager will again ask questions to clarify his suggestion. By digging behind ideas, the manager can get more than surface input. At the same time, the manager also becomes a role model for complete and quality listening.

Arynne SIMON SAYS:

It's more important for people to be heard, and for their ideas to be explored, than for you to actually use their ideas.

Listening to an idea doesn't mean
you are committing to it.
Quality listening doesn't infer that
you are agreeing.

Quality Questions: More on "Why"

This is where my earlier promise is kept. I promised to give you a further explanation for cautioning you against the 'why' question.

Some questions contain important qualities that allow them to be classified as 'quality questions.' 'Who,' 'what,' 'when,' 'where,' and 'how' are typical questions taught in most journalism classes to people studying how to write a news story. Yet many news writers these days have, unfortunately, added the 'why' question—which results in conjecture rather than fact. 'Why' seems to elicit lies, rationalizations, and excuses. So in my preferred list of quality questions, I never include 'why.'

'Why' questions hounded us through childhood; they carry messages of control and embarrassment, and memories of lies made up to avoid punishment. Words that evoke unpleasant memories of the past are not useful tools to use. Recently I told a group of parents that by using the word 'why' with their growing children, they could successfully train their kids to be expert liars in about six years.

Children, employees, everyone will always 'dream up' an answer when asked 'why.' Even executives and politicians, when interacting with the press, would do well to make it a rule never to answer a 'why' question—which, as you've already read in this book, is a question aimed to embarrass, trap or manipulate.

'Why' is a question that traps you into the back corners of life's playing field. And frankly, 'why' is a non-specific question used by people who don't know exactly what information they want. Amateur interviewers use it often, while the great interviewers like Ted Koppel and Hugh Downs never used 'why' unless they were out to make trouble for a guest. Barbara Walters used 'why' questions early in her career and got dramatic over-reactive responses from interviewees, making her the headlines that established her image. Later in her career, she rarely used this type of question.

'Why' is a question that makes people justify what they have done in the past. How much better to move life as quickly as possible into the language of the future: 'next time,' or 'in the future,' or 'let's do it this way.'

ARYNNE **SIMON SAYS:**

Life is best lived in forward drive.

There are many words that can be used as tools to dig for information. Among some worthy quality questions that you have already learned are 'who,' 'what,' 'when,' 'which,' 'how,' 'where,' 'is it,' 'can it,' 'does it,' or 'could it.' And there are many, many more that will get you solid facts and information rather than reasons, rationalizations, excuses, and lies. A question that gets you the information you want without putting another person off balance means that you know how to play the game of life. When you want information and you also want to protect a relationship, remember to use a quality question. If you want revenge or to make someone squirm, use 'why.'

Here's a workplace example that might be worth remembering. The situation is about a report turned in late. An angry manager barks, "Why is this late?" He then gets some frightened excuse that causes him to reassess his opinion of this person. If this manager truly wanted to grow the behavior of his people, he would be better off asking, "Where did this report get hung up? Is there something I could have done to help it get completed on time?" By asking specific questions, he has a chance to learn what might be done better the next time.

He might also ask, "In the future, if something is not going to get done on time, would you be willing to let me know beforehand?"

There are plenty of quality questions that will help a manager know how something can be prevented from happening again. But I chose this example to show how a manager gets out of Center Court because a report is late, and then how he uses the 'why' word as revenge. This manager has not yet learned an effective leadership style of communicating.

Remember the father who said he listened to his son. Had he asked only a few questions like, "What university back East seems to have the best climate for the sports you like," he might have found out something more than that his son wants an Eastern college. And more importantly, the son would have had the impression that his feelings were being heard, rather than just his information getting through.

But it takes both patience and courage to listen. Winston Churchill once said, "Courage is the understructure of all virtues." Churchill also said that "It takes courage to speak your mind, but it takes even more courage to listen." It may seem strange to you, but I have always thought that listening takes special courage, especially when someone is saying things you don't want to hear. It's important to be able to hear what others say, and to acknowledge that their thinking is worth hearing. If you hear something worthwhile, it might mean changing your mind—and that takes the greatest courage of all.

It's all too easy to brush aside the ideas of others or find fault with their logic. Many people need to disagree or disrespect the thoughts of others to feel justified to do it their own way.

I know a man who was drummed out as president of his company. He was sure that only his ideas were good ideas. This was a very intelligent man, and his ideas would have helped the company. But he never listened to anyone else, never acknowledged their abilities, and actually belittled people who spoke up at meetings by saying things like, "That's a damned fool idea." I never heard him ask a single quality question. This man used words as weapons, embarrassing people and pushing them into corners. It didn't take long before his appearance at the podium for a company communications meeting brought stomping and boos from a savvy but usually well-behaved work force.

This would-be leader suffered from untrained listening skills. He never learned that questions are the most powerful tools of leadership. The higher up the corporate ladder I work, the more questions I hear.

Question Caveats

However, there are a few caveats when it comes to asking questions. One or two won't throw the control balance off kilter, but the power of quality questions can throw a relationship off if you ask your manager or a client too many.

On the other hand, when it comes to people who work for you, ask as many as you'd like. The same goes for your peers. At home, try to balance your communications between giving information and asking questions. You'll be delighted to see the quality of all conversations improve as a result of interesting questions.

Questions can also be used as protective devices. If someone hits a button or throws you off balance, reach for a question. For example, in the supermarket when the cashier says, "No way—a twenty dollar bill? That's the third one in a row." Don't make a statement. Ask a quality question like, "Will you be able to get change for me?"

When someone makes as sarcastic remark about your Hawaiian shirt and you feel embarrassed, ask a question.

He says: "A purple shirt! Wow, aren't you the fashion plate." You respond with: "Have you ever owned anything in purple?" This method is like the high lob shot in tennis. The other player has to move around to return your lob, giving you time to get back in balance and think of something else to say. If you're still not in balance, ask another question—hit another lob.

Quality questions will become an effective part of your assertive communication skills. As soon as you learn to use these skills (including quality questions), you'll be playing life Center Court. Then you can encourage others to play life in Center Court with you.

EMOTIONAL FITNESS EXERCISES

1. Draw your own Three Box diagram on your computer and on your PDA. Refer to the diagram when you are on the phone, answering emails or at meetings.

2. Take a problem that may still be bothering you, and decide what you'd like to have as result when it's resolved. Form this into a sentence and consider it as your Box 3.

Now describe the situation or make up a sentence for Box 1.

State a fact for Box 2. Now read 1, 2, & 3.

And imagine someone answering you back.

Design another 1, 2, 3. (Remember that each time you come back to what you originally said you want.)

Did you try to make these three statements into a logical progression? If so, go back and say them without any joining words.

3. Take the first opportunity you can to put this new skill into practice.

4. Reread this chapter and be sure you understand it.

5. Draw question marks on pads around your desk and on scrap papers. Do this at meetings and when you are on the phone. Use these as reminders that you're going to ask questions, especially when someone is trying to put you on the spot. Pretend you are going to be a television interviewer of high caliber. (But remember, no 'why' questions.)

6. Talk to someone close to you, and find out two new things about how they think and how they came to take up some hobby or other.

7. Use at least once each day the following question: "What is your thinking on the subject of _____?" Just absorb their ideas and be determined not to have any come back. Let it go.

8. Before your next meeting, prepare a few questions on subjects you know will be brought up.

NOTE: I would like to suggest that among the best questions to ask at work begin with 'how' or 'when.'

11

On Being Comfortably Disliked

ARYNNE SIMON SAYS

**Hooray—
They dislike me!**

Emotionally healthy people strive for a better life, a successful life without discomfort. This is a natural part of the way healthy human beings function. So when you make someone else's life even the least little bit uncomfortable, how do you think they feel about you? Do they like you? No way! They do not like you. You may have decided not to notice their negative feelings but you are, indeed, *disliked.*

There was a time when child psychologists advised parents to say to their children, "I don't dislike *you;* I just dislike what you're doing." But it's my experience, both as a professional and from bringing up my own children, that we dislike even our children when they do things that cause discomfort.

I suggest you accept the fact that you will dislike, at least for a while, people who make life unpleasant for you. And I hope you will not let your very natural, human feelings escalate into guilt or shame.

131

We'll Do Halloween After Breakfast

One October, my daughter and I decided that we could buy two pumpkins for carving; the time had arrived when she was old enough to handle one on her very own. She'd outgrown the stage of watching mommy or daddy do the carving. So this year, before Halloween officially arrived, my husband and I agreed to promote her from being in charge of pumpkin seeds; she could design the pumpkin face and manage the knife. She was, indeed, excited at the prospect of creating her very own Jack O' Lantern.

I announced plans to get started on Saturday morning, before the family got caught up with the chores of the day. When I came down to start breakfast, I found that our excited daughter had already set up the kitchen table for the pumpkin project. She had spread newspapers, set up utensils—obviously eager to begin. But I had arranged in my mind that we'd all have breakfast first. I explained, "This is not yet the time for pumpkins—first we'll have breakfast and then after breakfast we'll do Halloween." She looked at me angrily and shouted, "I hate you. You ruin everything." Then, still in pajamas, she got her bike and pedaled down the driveway before I could even think to blame her behavior on emerging hormones. She was too young for that excuse. I was furious.

Clearly, things were off to a bad start on a day when there were so many Saturday chores to get done—not even counting the pumpkins. I cleared the newspapers and knives off the table, got breakfast ready and stopped her on the road in front of our house. "It's time for breakfast," I said. She replied, "I'm not having breakfast with you—I don't even want to look at you." I managed to shout after her as she rode away, "We better get breakfast out of the way so we can get you to your music lessons and still get the pumpkins done." I also made sure she heard: "I'm furious at you, too."

Waiting until she was pedaling back in my direction, I stopped her long enough to say, "Look, you don't like me right now, and I don't like you either. We have pumpkins to do. Believe it or not, people can work side by side disliking each other."

That surprised her enough that she responded, "You mean I can work near you and still dislike you?"

"Yes," I said, "it's done all the time in business. Our disliking each other won't last forever."

So she agreed to come inside, although we both continued to scowl at each other. By the time we had bought the pumpkins and were back scooping out the insides, she turned to me and said, "I like you now, Mommy." But I hadn't gotten over my annoyance, so I replied, "Well, I still dislike you." And that caused her to flare up again with, "I dislike you worse than I did before."

By the time we were finishing up and admiring each other's creative work, we liked each other again, and we both said so. Our daughter learned some lessons from that pumpkin experience that still come in handy; they are lessons that will be important when she has her own children or manages people—both positions sure to win dislike quite regularly.

The lessons she learned are that:

- People dislike each other, but it doesn't last forever;
- People who dislike each other can work side by side;
- Even nice and smart people sometimes dislike each other;
- Disliking is different from hating;
- Disliking does not have to be reasoned away; like the fog off the ocean, in time it just lifts.

Even Small Discomforts Lead to Dislike

If you make someone uncomfortable, even very briefly, they dislike you. Count on it! If you bump someone accidentally in the market, for a split second the person dislikes you. If you unintentionally knock something over in a friend's home, he/she dislikes you at that moment. But 'disliking' doesn't mean that you are hated enough to be punished or rejected.

It's amazing that the words 'hate' and 'revenge' are used so often by people very close to you. These words are emotionally charged, automatic words that don't accurately describe the simple dislike people are often feeling when they use the stronger language. The emotional terms are intended to make sure you get the impact of what's being said. People shout or use offensive, exaggerated language to be sure that their message is getting through.

Arynne **SIMON SAYS:**

When people express their anger in words, they want assurance that you've heard them and 'get it.'

Let people know so they 'get it,' but it would be better if you translated words like 'hate' into the basic word 'dislike.' Your partner may have said, "I hate you and I hate our life with you working all the time!" But it would be better if you answered, "I hear you. I know you dislike me for not planning weekends better." Notice how you have de-escalated the language in hopes that the feelings will also calm down.

'Dislike' is a very important word, one not used often enough. I suggest you substitute 'dislike' for other words that dramatize feelings. In the heat of anger, it is quite typical to use words that exaggerate feelings. Even in telling the story of an argument to a friend, people tend to say, "he hates me," "he can't stand me," "he'd like to kill me."

Arynne **SIMON SAYS:**

The word precedes the feeling.

"The word precedes the feeling" is a truism I often repeat. When you say, "My life is a total mess," it's nearly impossible to know how to begin organizing your life so it works. When you say, "I hate this work," the annoyance you have will grow into hating. To call a child a loser may, indeed, transform the child into one.

Many people are afraid of public speaking because they may have had an on-stage experience that caused them, as children, to be *excited*. The youngster was *excited* until some adult gave the feeling the incorrect description by saying, "You're *nervous.*" And for the rest of one's life, any stage or podium is linked with nervousness.

So stay in Center Court by being clear and accurate with the words you use to describe feelings. Use 'dislike' instead of 'hate,' and 'enjoy' rather than 'love.' *Enjoy* films with happy endings, rather than I love them. *Enjoy* chocolate rather than loving it. *Enjoy* mountain vacations and stop *hating* New York. You are free to dislike the big cities of the world and prefer holidays in nature, but you will come to feel the hatred if you speak it often enough.

Begin by concentrating on speaking simply, without dramatic exaggeration. Rather than hating a book, describe it as one that you would not recommend. Dislike eggplant rather than hating it. You will build the habit of using the word *dislike* if you begin first to express disliking inanimate things: "I *dislike* steaks that are under-done," or "I *dislike* wearing a yellow shirt to work." Soon it will become comfortable to express that you *dislike* "films with gratu-itous sex," or "books that have obvious endings," or "people who are too bossy"—and so on. You might even get to the place where you can say "I dislike myself when I do too much procrastinating."

Soap operas are dramatic; life is not meant to be dramatic. Your language about life situations would improve if it were plain and simple—even close to boring. Save all exaggerations for that screen-play or novel you're writing, the acting class you're going to take, the drawing or painting you're working on. Don't transform your life into a soap opera.

A friend of mine in New Jersey described her house after a heavy rain storm as "floating away." She said that she could "drown in her basement." But after a few questions, I determined that there was about an inch of water on the basement floor, and that she had already moved all the items in danger onto shelves. This friend was a soap-opera actress—not just in her overblown description of the water in her basement but in real life—and she was given to living every day as a drama.

But I have found that people too often think of their lives in extreme terms and describe them with great commotion. "My life is a total mess" is something psychologists hear too often.

Plainly there are daily situations in which you are disliked. Much of the time you're not aware of it. If you absent-mindedly stray into the adjacent lane of traffic on the highway, you could look in your rear-view mirror and see the dislike registered on the face of the driver you cut off. But unless this driver suffers from road rage, his dislike doesn't last very long. Every time you ask somebody for something that puts them out a little, they dislike you. I want you to be aware of this dislike, consciously aware that it does exist, and also aware that when others make you uncomfortable, you dislike them, too.

When you separate 'dislike' from 'hate,' you will not shy away from being disliked. Actually, it's possible to become proficient at anticipating when someone is going to dislike you, such as when you tell someone how you want a job done, ask for change in a shop without buying anything, or tell a friend that you would prefer to stay home rather than go out to dinner. You'll learn to accept dislike without your well-being suffering.

Give Your Children the Right to Dislike You

Very few parents are capable of saying forthrightly that they dislike their children—even for a brief time. Parents have been brainwashed to believe in unconditional love. But all a child has to do is look at the parents' faces to know how they really feel.

Everyone seeks acceptance and love; the search is especially frenetic in these times of divorce, drugs, terror, and insecurity—but what few people recognize is that without the freedom to dislike one another, no true love is possible.

I believe it's absolutely necessary for parents to give their children the license to express disliking them. The parent may say to a very small child who is misbehaving, "I dislike you, but I love you anyway." With an older child who is secure in his parents' love, it's not necessary to add the extra words.

By now you know that I view the word 'dislike' as a beautiful word. Its accuracy, poignancy and truthfulness intrigue me. But unless you are in Center Court, it's nearly impossible for you to absorb or feel this basic emotion. I would like you to give your children, your friends, and your significant others the freedom to dislike you. If they don't have your permission to feel and express disliking you, they will one day need to demonstrate it to you. All people—and that does include children—need a way to be sure that you know they sometimes dislike you. Dislike comes and goes, even while underlying feelings of love and respect remain intact.

Let People Get Over Disliking You by Themselves

Okay, I hope I've convinced you that it's very important for people to have the space to dislike each other. Now I want to convince you not to try to talk someone out of disliking you.

Don't sit at the edge of your child's bed and say, "You really shouldn't feel this way. I'm a good mommy (daddy). Look what I did for you yesterday—I took you to the playground / bought you a sweater / played ball with you."

Trying to talk anyone out of disliking you is effectively telling them they don't have the right to their feelings—you rob them of the right to dislike. Negative feelings don't always have a logical reason to exist, but they are part of what a healthy person does to establish independence.

Remember the lessons my daughter learned in the pumpkin episode: that even nice people have the right to dislike each other; that they cannot talk each other out of the dislike; that it's possible to work with someone you dislike; and that dislike goes away all by itself, without anybody really doing anything about it. As a matter of fact, if you do try to talk someone out of their dislike, the feeling of dislike will last longer and may be intensified. I suggest that you remind a child (and yourself): "I know you dislike me now. It won't last forever."

When people become aware of their feelings of dislike, they don't harbor guilt about how they feel, they don't quit jobs because they dislike someone at work, they don't avoid certain situations or people, because they know the uncomfortable feeling will eventually just fade away.

So, to stay in Center Court, just let it go—give people the space to dislike you. Tomorrow changes everything. If not tomorrow, the day after tomorrow.

It Won't Last Forever

A few years ago there was a lady I knew socially who didn't like me. She didn't want to talk to me, and her children and husband shrugged their shoulders in embarrassment. I didn't know what had happened or what I'd done to cause her to dislike me, but I let it alone.

A full year later, I met her at a party and had a chance to speak to her alone. I said, "You know, you've disliked me for a year now. I'd like to be your friend. Are you ready?" She replied, "I'm ready." That was all. Rather than go over the details of why she didn't like me—which is what women do sometimes and get themselves angry and hurt—I let it alone. Another example of giving people the space to dislike you. They'll get over it. Have confidence in the fact that they do get over it.

Arynne SIMON SAYS:

We all dislike each other at times, and the magical words to remember are: "It won't last for very long."

People Who Don't Want You to Change

There may be some individual in your life who will be unable to accept changes; even positive, wonderful changes in your life. As you develop emotional fitness skills, they may feel threatened and not want to continue the relationship with you. I had a close friend who could not handle the changes in our manner of relating as I became more open and direct. Without my being aware of it, we had some sort of a dysfunctional script, and as my role changed, she couldn't relate to me the way she was accustomed to. She refused to change. I tried to reassure her, but she couldn't adapt so she put me out of her life. This isolated instance is very unusual—you will often find that if you take your time and allow a person the freedom to dislike you, he will soon be your friend again and caring about you in a much less dependent way. Most people will take your cue and grow along with you.

Give yourself a pat on the back whenever you use the word *dislike*.

You get two pats on the back if you remember to think, "But it won't last for very long."

EMOTIONAL FITNESS EXERCISES

1. Think back to situations in which you were disliked. Make a list of things you've done to make people dislike you. Perhaps you called someone on the telephone early on a Sunday morning and woke them up; you may even have heard the dislike in the person's voice. If you've been practicing the exercises in the "Building Your 'No' Muscle" chapter, you know that you're disliked when you've asked for something that puts someone out.

2 For the rest of today, or beginning tomorrow, try to see dislike on the face of someone who you made (inadvertently) feel uncomfortable. Say to yourself, "That person dislikes me, but it won't last for very long."

3. Look around your environment (house or office) and make a list of the things you dislike about it. Don't say, 'I hate this; I hate that.' Change your language by using the word 'dislike.'

4. If you have the opportunity in the next few days to dislike someone close to you, say to him or her, "I dislike you now. It won't last for very long." Then when you've gotten over it, say, "I don't dislike you anymore; in fact, I love you (or I care about you, or want to get back together again)." Use the words "It won't last forever," and "I don't dislike you anymore."

12

Eliminating the Crazy-Makers

Arynne SIMON SAYS

When the emotions fight the intellect, the emotions always win.

Double Signals present a fiendish difficulty in life, primarily because most people are not aware that they even exist. Double Signals are crazy makers that drive you out of Center Court and prevent you from realizing your goals. They cause serious arguments, stress, and unhappiness.

The number twelve has always been my lucky number, so I selected Chapter 12 as a perfect place to write about the insidious nature of Double Signals; I will also include suggestions about how to overcome their impact on your life. Without understanding how to eliminate the crazy makers, you cannot play life in Center Court, you cannot be emotionally fit, you cannot have a reliably effective relationship.

In the days when all cars had gear-shifts, people learned to drive by coordinating the gas pedal with the clutch pedal, and the road test for a driver's license included getting started from a full stop on

141

a hill. If you managed to move your car forward without rolling backwards, it would get you a license plus a euphoric sensation of having demonstrated holding power over opposing forces.

Comic book adventures often threatened the hero with being squashed between opposing forces, like two walls closing in or the floor and ceiling coming together. In life, there are often occasions when we have a sense of opposing forces closing in on us like that, or else tearing us apart. Double Signals keep you from functioning unless you become aware of when this is happening to you. Yes, you can gain control over the 'gas and clutch pedals;' it requires becoming aware of being trapped between conflicting messages. But if you don't even recognize when opposing forces are at work in your life, you are in what I call a 'crazy-making' situation that can drive you back into the dark corners of Anger and Fear.

Trapped Between Anger and Fear

Recall the racquetball court illustration in Chapter One that demonstrates how anxiety builds when you race back and forth between the corners of Anger and Fear. It's much better to play life from either the Angry corner or the one called Fear, rather than run between the two. The problem is that Anger and Fear seem to act as dysfunctional partners; Anger generates Fear, and Fear seems to promote Anger.

People have asked me, "Which one is better, Anger or Fear?" I have concluded, much to the upset and disagreement of some, that it's better to be angry than fearful. Fear acts in ways that paralyze action, and so I suggest that anger may be—between the two—the better choice for the average person. It's better to be angry at a doctor than paralyzed with fear over an ailment. I have written the chapters on fear and catastrophizing to help quiet your fears, but it's the human destiny to learn to walk hand-in-hand with fear. People who have deep faith in a religion are essentially learning to cope with their fears in a beautiful way.

Anxiety is the combination of Anger and Fear that causes you to toss and turn in bed until you feel as if you're stumbling down the hillside of life. On your right side you think angry thoughts—"I shouldn't have said that to him in the interview." You shift to the

other side where the fearful thoughts are waiting to pounce—
"What if I don't get the job and he gives it to someone else?"

"I should have made a better presentation! What if he doesn't call
back?! I should have been more positive! What if my money runs
out before I get a job?" As you toss and turn between emotions of
Anger and Fear, you are disconnecting your brain and functioning
completely on your emotions. No wonder you feel wiped out in the
morning and have difficulty getting your work done.

The best way to get out of an anxiety state is to undo either the
Anger or the Fear, encouraging your brain to start working again.
Do not wear out your emotions during sleepless nights. It's far bet-
ter to get up and write a letter or find some work or a book to reac-
tivate your brain.

There are other traps, some self imposed, that threaten your emo-
tional orderliness during a lifetime. For example, if you want to take
a trip but your imagination kicks in with negative images, you are giv-
ing yourself some crazy-making Double Signals. You want to go to
Morocco, but your imagination writes a scene of you being caught in
a terrorist raid, hijacked in a plane or bus, captured as a hostage.
You're planning a camping trip to Yellowstone Park, but you begin
to imagine horrendous encounters with bears, murderers, storms,
and hazardous helicopter rescues. You want the promotion, but
imagine rejection and failure. Which is reality? It's your choice.

I recognize that most people were trained to stay aware of nega-
tive possibilities. Well-meaning parents give their children a daily
dose of Fear as though it were a vitamin pill, hoping to protect their
children against perilous realities. As a child, if you ran enthusiasti-
cally toward the swings in the playground, the voice of a loving par-
ent may have followed you. "Not too high. Don't stand too close to
others. You could have your teeth kicked out. Be careful."

Those childhood lessons continue to impose themselves on your
life now, keeping you from taking risks or even from trying new
things. If you have become "risk averse," perhaps you can recognize
that you are trapped in the lessons of your past. Whenever you hear
yourself think, "what if...," think of that child on the playground.

"This is a good real estate investment, but what if I can't afford
the payments a year from now?" "My sister is getting married in
Cleveland, but what if I get on the airplane and there's a terrorist

on board?" "The play group offered me a big role in their new pro-
duction, but what if I get on stage and can't remember my lines?"
"My boss wants me to give a speech at the industry conference, but
what if I'm so nervous that I make a fool of myself?"

The powers of your imagination are amazing—but they can be
destructive if they rob you of calm and pleasure.

Friendly warnings of possible catastrophes can also ruin your plans
or enjoyment. There are times you haven't thought of all the possible
things that could go wrong, but there is surely a parent, friend or doc-
tor who is all too ready to give you some fanciful ideas. The television
news is also a good source for generating unnecessary fears. Double
Signals lie in wait everywhere, and unless you recognize them as crazy-
makers, you will not be in charge of your own emotions.

Double Signals Wear Loving Masks

During the school year, my little daughter was at times awakened by
her father urging her to "Get up now; you overslept. It's 7 a.m., and
the carpool will be here at 7:30! Hurry!" On the days when her
Mickey Mouse alarm clock failed to penetrate her Disney dreams,
she'd jump out of bed, dress rapidly, and rush into the kitchen to
gulp down her breakfast.

Then I'd come on the scene and say to her, "Don't eat so fast: It's
not good for your stomach." One parent was telling her to "hurry,
hurry," and the other was saying, "slow down." This is a typical
Double Signals situation for children—conflicting orders bombard-
ing them from opposite directions. They have a sense of blowing up
over it. And one day she did. She pushed the Rice Krispies—milk,
bowl, and all—onto the floor. The Crazy-Makers had gotten to her.

As soon as I recognized the Double Signal I was giving my daugh-
ter by telling her not to eat so fast, I learned to say that it would be
better to eat more slowly, but eating fast once in a while wouldn't do
her any harm.

To Save or Not to Save

To have fresh-smelling clothes, an ecology-minded woman wanted to
hang her laundry outdoors instead of using a clothes dryer. Her

neighbors complained about the unsightly view of printed sheets and pink underwear visible from their windows. Like many of us these days, this housewife was hit with a community Double Signal: Save energy but don't pollute our view. She was "caught between a rock and a hard place"—another set of words to describe Double Signals.

Double Signal from the Judge

A young couple wheeled a box containing a damaged antique table into a small claims courtroom. The table had been ruined during shipment but, because the damage was not apparent from outside, they had signed for the delivery. Now the couple was seeking more recompense than the nine cents a pound the shipping company was required to pay in such a case. In his ruling, the Judge made a long, detailed argument against government regulations governing interstate carriers. But in the end, he had to abide by the current law, and the couple lost their case. The Judge told them as they were leaving—with the wife in tears—that they could take their case to the court of public opinion: in other words, complain to their friends about the injustice of the law. "You're right, but there's nothing the court can do." Double Signals in court are a common occurrence.

How Long Is a Kiss

Crazy Makers quite often find their way into a loving home. For example: While preparing dinner, a young mother is busily chopping onions and peppers, and trying to keep the kids occupied until mealtime. When her husband comes into the kitchen and gives her a long, sexy kiss, she'd like to be able to show affection. But his kiss has caused her to suffer the emotional pain of a Double Signal. Fighting an impulse to kiss him back, she also wants to push him away with her onion-scented hands and gruffly say, "Not now! The kids! Can't you see I'm in the middle of fixing dinner!"

So this lovely lady explodes in a most unexpected and unpleasant way as a result of the two conflicting demands surfacing at the same time. Women often feel trapped between the many roles as cook, lover, housekeeper, nurse, chauffeur, mother, etc. It's natural to resent the intrusion and imposition, when operating in one role, of having the feelings of another thrust onto you.

This woman's husband would be wiser to keep his kisses to a loving peck on the cheek rather than reveal his bedroom feelings in the kitchen.

When a Boss Is Not a Boss

A senior executive is expected to give orders and instructions and make demands. There is always a sense of something going wrong when a typically high-powered manager approaches his team and 'requests' they stay a bit later than usual. If he comes close to begging for their cooperation, it's conceived as a warning that something is not right.

A company asked me to put some strategies into place for a merger. The company that was acquired had had many tough managers, and the engineers were so used to this mode of behavior that I had trouble understanding the situation. They were unwilling to deal with or respond to a senior manager of the acquiring company, one of the kindest and most fair of men.

After looking into the situation, I realized that these employees didn't trust his "niceness." They expected direct communication, and he was asking permission rather than telling them what to do. His title said "BOSS"; his communication style said "FRIEND." Another double signal that needed to be explained.

What Are You Selling? Crazy Makers!

A size-twelve woman, who just started another diet, goes to the mall. The Barbie-shaped window mannequins display size four fashions, and she's tempted to try something on. But before she can ask if something comes in a size 12, she's tempted in another direction by the smell of food. Everything she loves is available, from sushi to fried chicken. She wants to stay on her diet and wear an eight, but all around her are food signals. "Thin is beautiful," says the mannequin. "You deserve a treat," says the food. Another crazy day at the mall.

Teenagers in shopping centers face other dilemmas. The hot merchandise aimed at the youth market is endless. But youngsters don't have enough money to satisfy all their CD, high-tech and clothes cravings. When the temptations get overwhelming in response to all the stimulation of things to buy, sometimes the temptation becomes overwhelming and shoplifting happens. Teenagers alone in a shopping center with this set of Double Signals often can't overcome the crazy-making situation. Parents or role models are needed to help the brain kick into action when the emotions swing out of control.

Emotions Are Stronger than the Brain

As soon as you experience a Double Signal and the emotions take over, the brain doesn't have a chance. That's why the Emotional Fitness exercises in this book are so important—to keep your brain polished and sharp, so that it understands what's going on and can stay in charge.

I surely don't want to completely squelch your playful and intuitive emotions. I know that people who make brain decisions about everything can become hard to deal with, and I don't want you to be like that. The trick is to allow the emotions to work, but keep the brain aware so that the emotions don't completely take over. Driving through life is something like driving down the freeway; looking ahead through the windshield, but glancing occasionally in the side view mirror. That's an adequate description of being emotionally fit.

Like the side view mirror, your emotions are adjustable. They can be fit into your life, yet still not overpower your brain. It's important to keep your emotions at the correct power level for the speed you're going. Not all counselors and coaches know how to do this—to help you keep this balance.

People are not perfect, and I'm not setting you up to expect perfection, but I want you to be aware of what causes you and those around you to feel like the walls are closing in—what causes you to flare up in sudden anger or frustration. Little children throw temper tantrums. They lie on the floor and kick and scream. This is probably the result of some Double Signal they've gotten. We adults sometimes wish we could have tantrums, too. In reality, we do.

How to Deal with Double Signals

As you learn to identify Double Signals, you will see them all around you—on television, in advertising, in your personal life. You'll be amazed at how many and how powerful they are, how many of them you're falling victim to, and—worse—how often you double-signal yourself. As you have already learned, most people do a real number on themselves by using the 'what if' statements.

To deal with the problem is to recognize what's happening. Then, when you are able to identify Crazy Makers and Double Signals, you'll want to learn what to do about them. That's my cue to write about the language skills that will set you up to combat the helplessness you feel when you are in the tangle of Double Signals.

Companies Can Be Crazy Makers, Too

Without understanding how they impact productivity, some businesses these days impose the ill effects of Double Signals on their employees. Very top management wants quality work and long term image/brand building, while across the company managers are being bonused on short term (quarterly) sales. Top level managers make speeches at communications meetings that emphasize attention to customers (customer intimacy, staying close to the customer, etc.). They claim to want service and support as a primary initiative. Meanwhile, across the company, service budgets are cut. CEO's speak of the need for loyalty, and then issue notices of headcount cuts. These are the frustrating dilemmas that executives must deal with. Companies that speak and act in a synchronized way do much better than businesses that impose Crazy Making on their employees.

Language Example #1: Dieters Deal with Double Signals

Successful dieting requires an advanced degree in dealing with Double Signals. At a buffet or cafeteria, the dieter faces a setting full of Double Signals. Many dieters don't enjoy parties because the temptation to go off the diet is so great: you can't get far enough away from that delicious-looking food, and you're constantly being encouraged back to the table. You say to yourself: "Those sardine sandwiches are filled with Omega 3 and only a few carbs. I can try one; it wouldn't hurt." At a potluck dinner, everyone implores you to try whatever "special new recipe" they've brought. The dieter attends a social gathering to have a good time, but finds himself/herself suffering as though being tortured.

If you are a dieter, it's important to realize what signals you're facing. I suggest you find the courage to say out loud to a few friends, "I'm on a diet. I want to stay on my diet tonight. Please help me stay away from the food, especially the desserts." It's necessary to verbalize what you want in this situation. *(To know what you want and have the courage to ask for it.)*

At home, leave a pencil and slip of paper at your place. At mealtime, it will help if you write down the words, "I want to stay on my diet and lose weight. I want this meal to be perfect." If you're eating with others, it would be better to say it out loud, as well. Don't say it quickly, nor as a joke; say it straight—"I'm on a diet, and this time I really want to lose weight. I don't want to go off my diet." This is more successful than keeping a food diary—and much easier. *(A good diet day is knowing our goal and having the courage to request help to achieve it.)*

In addition, I would still like you to get comfortable saying out loud what it is you want. It will feed back into your ears as a trumpet blast reminding you of what's important to you. Verbalizing will let others know you need their help. Speaking about your goal will give you the direction and determination you need. If you're asked out for a meal while on a diet, perhaps you can say, "Of course I want to have lunch with you. But I'm on a serious eating program, and I really don't want to be distracted from it. I wonder if you'd be willing to notice if I start ordering off my program." This verbalization of what you want will turn a dieting Double Signal into a single-message signal. Just thinking about what you want is not sufficient; you must express it verbally—out loud, or on paper. As long as the wants stay inside your brain, they're not being expressed as an intellectual statement. Thinking about something keeps it as an emotion—one which will not help you to stick to your goal.

Now you understand why making lists and writing goals are really important things to do.

Language Example #2: More About What to Say to a Loving Husband

If dieting seems a difficult place to begin your understanding and success in conquering the feelings involved with Double Signals, even more difficult are Double Signals involving other people—especially those who are close to you.

For instance, you've learned what a wife can say when she's experiencing an emotional explosion of anxiety produced by the Double Signal of onions and peppers and kids combined with her husband's sexy kiss. How does she say what she wants without rejecting her husband, who has come into the kitchen with more on his mind than food? Instead of saying "No" and pushing him away, she says what she'd like: "Two-second kisses in the kitchen."

But it's important that she understand the Double Signal that's causing her upset. A full version of what this woman can say is, "Everyone knows that love is the main ingredient of good food. Two-minute kisses in the kitchen make me crazy. When I'm cooking, I want two-second kisses."

You're right to think that no one could think up a response like this on the spur of the moment. But wait: the next time something similar happens, you'll have had a chance to think over the suggestions you've read here. You will, I hope, have done your fitness exercises, and will be able to deal with a Double Signal situation like this directly and comfortably. You might not want two-second kisses. You may want limits like, "In the kitchen, I like friendly pats." Or you'd rather reply, "Okay, send the kids to the neighbors and let's put dinner off until later."

It's *your* life; decide what *you* want, think about it, and then ask for it.

Most people don't understand where much of their anger comes from in close relationships. But once you recognize Double Signals at work, you can start using the technique I've described to avert the anxiety and handle many situations with a new found grace and ease.

EMOTIONAL FITNESS EXERCISES

1. For the next twenty-four hours, make a list of all the Double Signals you see.

2. Watch an hour's worth of TV and see how many Double Signals you find in the programming and the ads, as well as in your own mind. Write them down.

3. Analyze your relationship with someone with whom you don't get along to see how many Double Signals you can find in your feelings and the actions between you.

4. If you have a misbehaving child, search for the Double Signals that you are creating. (Even a tiny child having a tantrum may be suffering from Double Signal syndrome; see if you can analyze it and head it off.)

13

Giving and Taking Criticism

ARYNNE SIMON SAYS

No one takes criticism well; some people are just better actors—or perhaps they have taken one of my classes.

I t's now time to learn how to manage your feelings and behavior when it comes to criticism, discipline and put-downs. You have learned, and hopefully practiced, the skills that will be needed to stay in Center Court even when negative vibes are being hurled your way. Get ready to be surprised at how smoothly your new skills will lighten the emotional discomfort that criticism brings. Soon you'll feel much more comfortable with both the giving and receiving of criticism.

What Is Criticism?

Most often when people get angry and find fault with others, they are fundamentally annoyed with *themselves* for not having come to terms with what they want. The very act of blaming is best viewed as hacking one's way through a jungle of confusion, using angry words instead of a machete. When you finally discover what you really want, the blaming and anger disappear. Meanwhile, we very nice people have done considerable damage to those we've blamed or criticized harshly—often people we sincerely care about.

Since the source of blame and criticism comes from not knowing specifically what it is we want, most people go through dramatic crises, tearing into those around them. It's hard to realize that when we get into blaming others, we're getting close to discovering what we really want. So there is some benefit to the process of blame. But relationships can be damaged beyond repair or irreparably scarred because of this negative step along the path to getting to know ourselves.

In a business setting, for example, a manager might blame a direct report for taking a week to write a white paper that she wanted done in one day. When giving the assignment, the manager forgot to say, "I'd like this completed by 2 o'clock on Wednesday, and I'd like the style to follow the format used on this white paper that I did for my former company. If this can't be done by then, please let me know this afternoon, via email, how long you estimate it will take."

That's an example of the kind of very clear communication that sets someone up to succeed. It's the kind of communication from an experienced manager who is clear about what she wants, and knows how to let the other person understand her expectations. A novice manager couldn't determine how long this project takes, nor what process would best be followed. Not knowing how something is done, and how much time is appropriate for getting it done, always leads to dissatisfaction and blame. Experience can best be described as knowing how long an activity takes, how much it costs, and how it's most successfully done.

"Set the table" is the kind of non-specific request that will often lead to blaming a child for overlooking details. "I'd like the table set using place mats," is an improvement. Children and direct reports might complain of being "micro-managed," but there will be less opportunity for a parent or manager to criticize the work when it's done. "You never get me what I want for my birthday," translates better into "This year for my birthday I hope to get art supplies rather than clothing." Being precise about what you'd like will help people to succeed for you and eliminate much of your need to blame or criticize. And best of all, your relationships will, indeed, improve and succeed.

It would be better if you learn to thoughtfully and calmly realize that behind your dissatisfactions are often unexpressed things you want. Think of dissatisfaction as a huge rock, and what you really want is something hiding behind it.

Arynne SIMON SAYS:

Think of dissatisfaction as a rock—what you really want is hiding behind it.

It's quite important for you to understand that any behavior critical or blaming of others is a reminder to search harder for what it is you want. Then when you have found out what you really want, you must then find a way to express it appropriately. That second part—what to say—will be taught later in this chapter.

A good day is any day when you are clear about what you want and have the courage to say it. A good day is not a day when you demand getting what you want; that need to have things your way is called a tantrum. But I hope you will learn to stay in touch with what you want and develop the courage to say it to yourself, or better still, to another person.

Hearing Criticism

When someone criticizes you, think of it as the perfect chance to help that person find out what they want. A first step is to begin listening to what is essentially being said. What is it they want? If it's a boss who's criticizing you, it's very important to hear the criticism, as the boss is telling you how he/she wants something done differently next time.

The criticism a young person gets from his parents may hide their desire to know that he is safe from harmful outside influences. We tend to criticize our children instead of asking for reassurance. "You're so inconsiderate. You never call when you're going to be home late," instead of "Mom and I find it hard to sleep when you're out driving after 1 a.m. I wonder in the future if you could call to tell us where you are and that everything is okay."

The specifics of what you want often hide. Finding the source of a critical attitude, the real 'want,' may be like a young mother trying to find out why a baby is crying or misbehaving. She tries everything from changing diapers to a warm bottle to gentle rocking. She has to play detective in order to discover what the child wants. So from now on, you will hear all criticism, even criticism that's leveled at you in an unemotional way, as a form of anger that is trying to drive you out of Center Court. I'd like you to hear it as someone not knowing what they want and calling to you to help them figure it out.

But even if you're successful in changing how you set people up to succeed for you, you'll find that most people will continue to criticize. I know you can begin to hear criticism differently, understand it from a new point of view, and be able to handle it with the sophisticated knowledge of what's really behind the fault-finding. It will still give you pain, but managing your pain means you are pretty close to being in Center Court.

Criticism from Your Boss

Specifically, how do you respond if a boss criticizes you with a statement like "You're never accurate," or "You're a liar"? What is he trying to say? Based on what you've learned in this chapter so far, stop and consider for a moment and listen with your adult "third ear" to what your boss is really saying—what he would say if he were able to express himself more effectively. Perhaps something like, "I want information that's absolutely accurate. I want to be able to rely on the information I receive. I don't want to look like a fool by presenting information that turns out to be wrong."

As I've said, in some cases it's up to you to try to figure out what the person wants; at the same time, you're deciding whether or not the criticism is valid. If it is, you answer using the same pattern as before: "That's a valid criticism of me. I have a tendency to accept information from the first source without checking it. I'd like to go back and recheck this information, so you can rely on it."

If the criticism doesn't fit—if you are always accurate in your research—you might answer something like, "I turned this paper over to you after just an hour's work, but I *have* checked out all the information, so you can be confident. I would hope in the future to be considered dependable about research information."

Deciding on the appropriate response to someone who's criticizing you also has to do with whether this person is someone who can give you instructions. If the person does have that clout, you might decide that this is not the time to speak up.

But if you think that no one *should* give you this kind of harsh criticism, watch out. Remember that the 'should' will lead you to anger, and your words will reveal your feelings. Not a good idea! Words like 'lie' are designed to press your buttons and drive you into the corners of anger and fear. If you want the person to give you more specific instructions, you might say, "Accuracy is always important in business. It seems to me that you want even more current information. I'd like some specific directions so I can go back and redo the work."

Physical Stress Often Leads to Self Discovery

During physically uncomfortable periods in our lives such as illness, fatigue, or even pre-menstrual tension, people are, of course, irritable. They typically say disagreeable things that they would later prefer to retract. Friends, family and co-workers indulge the stress-ridden person until the mood is over.

Since physical discomfort takes you out of Center Court, during these periods you naturally make decisions or react in ways that are not quite the way you typically behave. But I'm not asking you to discount your 'moody' feelings altogether. In fact, staying aware of overreactions at a time of heightened sensitivity may actually bring you closer to an awareness of what it is you really want. Your behavior may be offensively over-reactive, but you are in a state of heightened awareness—often a keen time to discover important feelings. Sure, it would be better if you could do this without destructive words and behaviors. But try to remember that, somewhere amidst all the discomfort you feel and the pain you are causing others, there's a golden nugget of truth that can take you closer to knowing yourself and what it is you really want.

Here's a letter that express how illness can often serve as a growth experience.

Boy, was I a pain in the a-- to everyone during the 11 months I spent in bed trying to recover from an illness I'm still not sure was ever accurately diagnosed.

Having been blessed with health and energy all my life, I never even heard it when someone wished me good health; I just took good health for granted. Now I find myself really hearing every word when I'm wished a healthy year.

During those months I learned much about healthy eating and meditation and breathing. My kids are getting tired of my suggestions about food and fitness. I have finally allowed new age information from Drs. Mercola and Weil to make a positive impression on me. I am more open to asking people for help, and willing to think about helping others in a truly meaningful way. These days I usually know what I want and I have the courage to ask for it. I had too much time to practice what you suggest on your tape course. I am a changed person, better in every way.

In the past I sent flowers or books to friends who were ill and thought that made me a nice lady. But now I take the time to call and visit and find some way to be helpful. It took my own experience with being shut in to realize how dependent one can feel.

I have yet to regain my full strength, and I admit to procrastinating about joining a fitness center. But I thank my lucky stars that listening to your Emotional Fitness tapes came to my attention from a good friend who bought me them and a tape player instead of flowers. I bless her for it.

Getting Simonized really made a huge difference in how I treated the doctors, health care givers, friends, and family.

Getting to Know Yourself

A close friend, who is possessed of both an excessive amount of money and excessive poundage, has his elegant clothes made in France. The fabrics are luxurious and the workmanship superb; despite his size, many people admire, even covet, his wardrobe. He loves to give things away, but his size makes his offerings into a big joke; his shape is one that would have made Jackie Gleason feel skinny. Pound for pound, he would be considered a disaster by the American Heart Association.

But let's imagine for a minute that this man offers you a pair of his brand-new fantastic silk undershorts. My question to you is, would you take them? Would you, as he is insisting, even try them on? Is it possible that these silk boxers would fit you? The chances are that you're nowhere near as round as my friend is, and most likely you will say, "Thanks, but no thanks." You know perfectly well that even if you had them drastically altered, they would still be wrong for you. There's no sense trying on a pair of shorts, even silk ones with hand-sewn hems, when it's obvious they'd slip down around your ankles.

An interesting observation I've made about people who have a weight problem is that they cannot look at something and be sure if it will fit or not. They often try on clothes that are too loose or too tight, because they don't have an accurate sense of what they look like. Very small children have the same problem, and choose shoes or shirts that are meant for tinier kids. Recognizing one's correct size is often an indication of coming to grips with reality. When we begin to have a truer sense of ourselves physically, we become more clear and accurate in estimating the size that's right for our body. Learning to accurately estimate physical size and shape is one way of growing up (and a reason to take your kids shopping with you).

Okay, so you turned down the French silk shorts, and rightly so. After all, why waste your time trying on an item of clothing that you know won't fit? And I suggest you not take them to save for transforming them into a pillow or something else. There is too much else for you to do, so don't waste your storage space or creative time thinking up other ways to use the shorts.

Do you always take someone's advice, absorb their criticism, or use their suggestions? I hope not. Can you use the metaphor of the French undershorts to see where I'm going? If someone directs a critical remark at you, are you instantly aware of whether or not it's accurate? Do you really know yourself? Another aspect of growing up is being able to recognize if a criticism 'fits' you or not.

If somebody criticized me by saying, "You're always full of suggestions," I would know that statement is pretty accurate. So I might answer something like, "Yes, you're right. That description surely fits me a lot of the time." But if someone angrily said to me, "You know, you're a very self-centered lady," I'd be able to say with conviction, "No, I don't accept that. It's not a fitting description of me." When I was younger, I might have tried on the criticism to see if it fit. But at this point in my life, I make the final decision about whether the criticism is accurate or not.

If, on the other hand, a brand new pair of French silk undershorts were offered to me by someone pretty nearly my size, I might try them on to see if they fit. In the same way, if there is some element of truth in the criticism, I often hear myself saying, "Let me consider that—I'm not sure it's a good description of me. I'll think about it and let you know."

Know and Accept What You're NOT Good at Doing

There are varied concepts offered on how to build one's self confidence. Some coaches advise that self confidence is built by focusing on your many abilities, talents and strengths. But it's my view that, until you know and are willing to tell others what you don't do well, your confidence levels will not expand.

Being told how wonderful you are, how important, how capable, will help—but only to a limited extent. Being human, you are sure to be flawed in many ways. My patience levels have not always been what I would prefer; my ability to give driving directions leaves much to be desired, I collect too many papers on my desk and subscribe to far more publications than I can possibly read. I tend to over-teach, to need praise and be in the spotlight beyond what I think is reasonable. And the list goes on. Someone recently said to me, "Arynne, you over-do everything." I replied, "Thank you for noticing—that's an accurate description of me."

To play life in Center Court, you would do well to know what you can do and what you *cannot* do. Be sure your *Cannot* list is a long one; read the biographies of successful people and you'll find that they were interesting enough to require notice of both their virtues and their flaws.

Many people think that psychiatrists are trained to eradicate their problems by eliminating their faults. If you suffer from a serious problem such as extreme obsessive behavior, the problem certainly needs to be addressed. But a lesser flaw, one that doesn't interfere with your well-being, might be worth looking at clearly, finally accepting that it belongs to you. Lesser flaws can be dealt with in classes or by a psychologist, but basically your flaws are what makes you interesting. And your flaws, as well as your virtues, tend to increase as you grow older. For every new skill or virtue you add, you're bound to pick up a little dust along the way. If you decide to spend your life trying to hide or eliminate your faults, you'll spend all your time in various sorts of therapy, attending a string of self-help seminars, or using manipulative tricks to keep people from seeing you as you really are. Playing life in Center Court means accepting both your positive and negative qualities, and staying open to adding new ones.

It's possible that even your virtues might be criticized if they make someone uncomfortable. If you're a very fast, hard worker, that certainly is a virtue. But someone who has to work alongside you might be made uncomfortable if they're unable to keep up. A very neat, precise person who does everything accurately and on time can be a pain-in-the-a-- to someone who is constantly remind-ed of his own inadequacies. The virtuous giggle of a four-year-old becomes a flaw to a mother with a headache. If you're criticized for a virtue, hear where it's coming from and don't accept it. Smile as you might have done with my obese friend (the rich one) and say, "Thanks—but no thanks."

Arynne SIMON SAYS:

Don't accept criticism if it doesn't fit.

You've too often heard, "Don't take criticism personally." Criticism hurts—but you want to be able to accept it without getting put down. Until you understand how to accept criticism in terms of work to be done, your feelings are going to be hurt. Even if you're being criticized for something you know you're good at, you start to feel threatened. We're all very tender. Some people have a very dif-ficult time accepting criticism, but if you can see it instead as some-one telling you what they want, it's much easier to accept.

It's also helpful to reassure someone criticizing you that you don't dislike them for it. You can even help others out of the corners of Anger and Fear by saying something like, "That's a good idea. Why didn't I think of that?" A criticism is a form of someone giving you and idea or an instruction. Considering it is up to you.

ARYNNE **SIMON SAYS:**

Live life in forward motion; criticism and blame are designed to push you backwards."

When You Know How to Take Criticism, You'll Also Know How to Give It

The best way to deliver criticism is not as a negative that clobbers someone. Consider criticism as a form of giving directions for future behavior. Change the tense from past to future as fast as you can. Someone says: "You never reset the amount on the stamp machine." You reply, "In the future I think I would do better if there were a reminder on the stamp machine."

A creative person who contributes new ideas and out-of-the-box thinking to many tasks may be too laid back about the mundane details of schedules and record keeping. How can this boss best give directions to help this maverick be a more effective part of the work group?

He can do it by first acknowledging the employee's strengths, then stating what the requirements are for the work group or the business. "Some people prefer to use their brains creatively. You do that part of the work very well. It's important for me to track work schedules and other mundane details. I'm good at that, and I don't even mind the reports and paperwork. The vice president I report to counts on me to get my reports to him on time. I want the paperwork from everyone in the group to come in accurately and promptly, so I can get mine done accurately and promptly." The boss expresses his appreciation for this creative individual, and only after that does he say what he, as boss, wants in the particular situation.

By describing himself as someone who enjoys mundane paperwork, this boss is also teaching his creative employee to recognize and accept differences between employees...perhaps training him for a management position.

A Hint About Expressing Praise or Criticism

Words that describe any virtuous behavior can skillfully magnify the praise if they are offered in retrospect. And by using the past tense to express criticism, you can diminish and soften the pain that criticism inflicts. "Last week when you washed the car, I wasn't satisfied. Next time, I'd like the chrome polished so it really shines, and the dashboard given a dust-free treatment." Yes, you can learn to invest a few days as you wait to give criticism that will enhance, rather than smash, a relationship.

Arynne SIMON SAYS:

Use the past tense to soften the criticism and enhance your praise.

Challenge: How Would You Handle This?

Now that you have the principle in mind, I want to present a situation and let you decide on how you would handle it, then compare your solution to mine.

Here's the situation:

Your boss, Andy, is annoyed about having his messages scattered around the office on little bits of pink paper, and he's grown to feel dislike toward Susan, the assistant responsible. Typical of bosses who want everything done their way, Andy feels anger about the situation because he *shouldn't* have to put up with "foolish ways of doing things." (My way is the only right way.) And fear is part of this scenario as well. Telling Susan not to spread messages around will result in his being disliked, and maybe Susan will quit. In a state of Anxiety ('should' produces anger, plus fear of being disliked and possibly rejected), Andy blasts his criticism at Susan in an aggressive manner.

Put yourself in Andy's shoes. Based on the principles in this chapter and earlier in the book, how would you handle this?

One Answer

Here's my response to this, and one version of the wording I might use.

First, as you know, get rid of all 'shoulds' (Anger) and any catastrophizing (Fear). And then you'll use the Three Box method to say whatever you have decided to say—

Box 1: "Everyone would agree that this office works like a charm because of the support I get from my admins." Box 2: "It's difficult for me to keep track of messages on little slips of paper." Box 3: "I'd prefer a system that would have all the messages on one piece of paper, with action items clearly underlined."

This kind of communication proves that the boss has thought the problem out and has figured out what he wants. It starts with a Box 1 connection, then gives a reason, and then makes a statement of what's desired.

To the listener, this hardly sounds like a criticism; it sounds much more like a positive suggestion for the future.

When You Know What You Want, You Don't Criticize

One of the best benefits of getting emotionally fit is that it encourages you to get in touch with what you want. In any given situation, you'll learn to decide quickly what it is you want, and in doing so, you'll experience the amazing change in how people work for you. You will set people up to succeed. There won't be a need to criticize. Instead, you'll simply state what you'd like, want or demand, and of course you'll be prepared to accept a 'no.' The chances are, if you say want you want as clearly as possible, you'll hardly ever get a 'No.'

Instead of saying, "You're staying out too late," a parent in Center Court says, "If you're going to be home later than 12 (the agreed on time), Mom and I would like a phone call to reassure us that you're okay and tell us what time to expect you."

The boss says, "I want the company logo on all forms, even the ones for internal use," in place of "Nothing you people produce looks like we have a successful business."

Effective direction makes very clear what you'd like. If you don't know precisely what you want, it's a good indication that you would do well to look for someone, a mentor or coach or a course at a local college, to teach you. Consultants are worth their weight in gold if they can articulate the precision of their experienced thinking.

ARYNNE SIMON SAYS:

Don't tell others what they did wrong. Describe what you would like done in the future.

Popular love ballads seem often to be based on a dysfunctional, neurotic communication style—others being held responsible. "*You* made me love you. I didn't want to do it." "*You* went away, and my heart went with you." Sappy messages in songs and in life blame someone else for your feelings and hold others responsible for your happiness, comfort, or stability. In life we have the same complaints ourselves, and hear them from others. "*Your* personality is tearing me down." "*Your* bad moods are making me upset." "*Your* noise is driving me up a wall." "*Your* coming home late makes me anxious." "*Your* reckless spending is driving us to the poor house." "*Your* cooking is making me fat." The 'you' statement is particularly aggressive.

Putting the blame on others is emotionally flabby behavior. You are living life in the back corners of Anger and Fear if snobby salespeople cause you to buy things you don't need; if your boss puts pressure on you and you respond by eating too many candy bars; if the other kids are doing it so you have to do it, too. Listen to people who are blaming others, and know for sure that they are not in Center Court. Sure it's comforting to hold others responsible for your own shortcomings or unhappy predicament. So now and again you will revert to blaming the other drivers on the road for making you nervous and giving you a headache. But I don't want you to do that very often. I hope you have learned the skills you need to keep yourself in Center Court—or at least know when you are out of Center Court and find a way to get back there.

Instead of saying: "You made me love you," it would be better to say, "I was ready to love you after I saw how well you treat your mother." Save the 'you' messages for writing a hit song or movie; 'I' messages are better in life.

While you are learning not to blame others, you will most surely continue to be criticized. It's the only way most people know how to cope with what they don't like around them. Until they've been trained differently, critical behavior is the only way most people know how to defensively describe what it is that bothers them.

Consider harsh criticism as a form of brutality. Instead, you will clearly and precisely state what you'd like done. At first you will be criticized for your new directness. You might even have gotten everyone used to doing what you ask only after you have escalated the volume and the nastiness. It will take a while for the people around you to get used to your simply asking for what it is you want. And it will take a bit of work for you to come to grips with what it is you really want and just say it. But in time, people at home and at work will learn to hear you and will listen.

By then you'll be able to hear differently when other people criticize you. You will learn to be able to hear, lingering behind the complaint, what it is that the person really wants. Remember that the frustration that prompts people to launch into criticism can energize your brain to find solutions to problems. Criticism is a negative shortcut that obscures what is fundamentally wanted.

EMOTIONAL FITNESS EXERCISES

Don't be one of the people who give lip service to the saying 'Nobody's perfect.' Now is the time to write down what you think are your own imperfections. This is your list. Don't ask anyone for help with this exercise. The point of making a list you can print out or see is that, when you do write things down, you face them directly. Your flaws, as you see them, will become just another part of the reality of who you are. With this to back you up, you will be well prepared to accept criticism.

1. Make a list of any behaviors you can be criticized for. Be honest. Then memorize your list. This will prepare you to accept criticism from others. And if someone criticizes something already on your list, you'll know that "it fits." If you hear a criticism and it's not on your list, be ready to say, "That's not me. I don't think your criticism fits me at all."

   NOTE: Don't show your list to anyone. If they haven't figured out your shortcomings, you don't have to point them out. Let others uncover the mystery of the real you. If someone says, "You never respond to letters or emails," you can courageously say, "That's such an accurate description of me. I try to answer but never succeed. It would help if you would nag me about that."

2. You now know that it's far better to give suggestions or instructions (directions) instead of giving criticism. You also know that it's much more effective to leave out the 'you' when you want something done. Think of the many critical statements you typically make and reconstruct them. Here are a few examples. Make up at least five of your own.

   "Your room's a mess." *"I want the room picked up."*

   "Your work never comes in on time." *"I want the people on my team to stick to promised deadlines."*

   "Your ideas are impractical!" *"I would like numbers of cost and profit to be submitted with all ideas."*

3. Write a single paragraph that explains how you may be held responsible for something you had at one time blamed on someone else. Again, you do not share this information or do anything about it. Just write the paragraph. This simple exercise will strengthen an important muscle that you require for playing life in Center Court.

14

Expressing Anger

Arynne SIMON SAYS

**Anger expressed incorrectly has
widening rings of sad consequences.**

What can you do when your calmly assertive speech doesn't
seem to be getting through and you are, despite what you've
learned in this wise and wonderful book, building up a head of steam
that's about to culminate in a full blown case of anger? There are,
indeed, times when the expression of anger is absolutely necessary.

Wait a minute. *Expression* of anger is different than *feelings* of anger!
So you need to learn how to express anger efficiently—without dam-
aging other people—even though at the moment you might feel like
doing just that. It's wise to be prepared with a more powerful level of
speech when assertive language doesn't seem to be working.

Expressing anger can be specifically learned, for it is just another
behavior skill. It's quite obvious to everyone that when a parent uses
physical methods to act out their anger, the violence continues into
subsequent generations and often spreads into the community.

Verbal abuse is like throwing a pebble into a calm pool of water. Anger expressed incorrectly has widening rings of consequences. The ripple effect of abuse is well documented.

So unless the articulation of one's feelings is done appropriately, there is always a serious down side. In our enlightened age, many programs can help people discover who they are, and many training methods are available to help people learn how best to express themselves without doing damage to others, as this book is doing.

However, when you choose a coach, counselor or guru, it's vital to establish their values and not to go to someone whose values and ethics are not ones you admire. You and your counselor can disagree on politics and on styles of clothing, but it's wise to ask: does he/she respect the institution of marriage? The institution of religion? Does your counselor encourage retirement, or is the work ethic one they prefer? How about having children?

Psychologists are trained to help people rediscover themselves; they are not supposed to impose their own set of values. But it's like saying that members of the media are not supposed to be opinionated. Hollywood mogul Samuel Goldwyn gave the world a funny quotable when he said, "Anyone who goes to a psychiatrist should have his head examined." It's my opinion that anyone who goes to a counselor, coach, or psychologist without asking about the person's values should have his/her head examined.

Recently I witnessed a man "find" himself again by attending a seminar much touted by his many men friends. He had long been lost in a marriage to a rather controlling woman. The instructor, a Ph.D. in psychology, was successful in helping this man pick up the pieces of his life and reweave the threads. Yet one could say that the operation was a success, but that the patient died. Indeed, this man now has a new career and claims he's happier, but his marriage is over; he has lost his wife as well as her parents whom he liked quite well; his career of many years is gone and so are many of his old friends.

It seems that the seminar leader, who became his psychologist, has a skewed view on marriage, on male/female relationships, and on the American corporation as a worthy work place. Without doubt, this counselor convinces many people to his way of seeing the world. I consider it unfortunate that too many men sign up for his retreats, seminars and men-only sessions.

But Isn't Anger Necessary at Times?

Assertive language allows a wide variety of communication levels when you express your wishes or requirements. It's rather like using the gas pedal to go from 15 mph with 'I'd like' to 90 mph with 'I demand,' which comes very close to aggressively expressing anger. The intensity of your voice will also reflect the rising importance of your request. When a speed of 40 or 50 mph assertiveness isn't working, you might in fact try saying, "I'm angry and getting angrier."

But even shouting doesn't do as much damage to others as saying something like, "You get me so mad—you're an idiot." Instead you can say things like, "I wish I had the courage to leave." An extreme 110 mph is rarely necessary. Threaten if you have no other way—but never, never, never use the word 'you.' "I will call 911." "I will find a way to make this message heard or I will leave." Note the absence of 'you' in all properly effective angry communication.

Your anger will leak out from time to time. Like a burp, it's neither very harmful to society nor to a relationship. But if you feel great amounts of anger on a regular basis, it's much better to have professional counseling on anger management.

Look for a group like the one in Los Angeles I've mentioned earlier, Talk Works, that offers specialized counselors to lead you through transitions. When you're going through a life transition, you can use help learning how to handle the situation until things settle down. Of course, I suggest you try first to dissipate your own anger in ways you've been taught in this book, either by yourself, or with a friend, or with a counselor.

Give voice to your anger in non-dramatic tones. Analyze your 'shoulds' to get rid of most of the angry feelings before you attempt to deal with whatever touched off the reaction. As long as you are feeling anger, there is no way to deal effectively with the problem. It's up to you to de-escalate the feelings and get into Center Court before speaking or acting. You can do it. You will do it if you have followed the exercises in this book.

Many close relationships bear ugly scars or are irreparably damaged by free and frequent expressions of anger. No wonder people want to divorce and start over; they can't abide facing the emotional scars they caused to someone who was once precious to them. Rather than face the scars we created, we leave the old relationship behind to start afresh. But soon, if you haven't learned how to express anger from Center Court, the new relationship will bear the scars of verbal violence

Express Anger in the Past Tense

Of course it's sometimes important to express anger. The question is how and when.

ARYNNE SIMON SAYS:

If you feel it today, express it tomorrow.

Don't even think I'm suggesting that you forget your anger or what caused it; I would never suggest that you 'bury' it. However, I advise that anger is best expressed in retrospect. For example, you can say to an employee, "Yesterday I was very angry when I heard the way that customer was talked to." Putting anger into the past tense doesn't do damage to another in quite the same way as getting angry at the moment when all feelings are on the surface and everyone is vulnerable. The incident will not have been forgotten in a day or two or three, but the emotions of shame and guilt will have quieted, leaving the expression of your remembered anger to be heard by someone's brain instead of by a heart in turmoil. And so you might have a better chance at getting through.

After you've successfully stayed in center court for a while, it's quite possible that you'll reap the benefits of a new, in-charge behavior. You'll be playing the game of life from center court. You will have expressed your anger, but without hurting another person and scarring the relationship.

Yes, I'm suggesting that you express the emotion of anger in an intellectual style. Very laid back. Not dramatic in any way. This may sound like a terribly phony way of dealing with people, but it's far less brutal. You've observed enough about interpersonal relationships to understand the reasons why letting your full feelings out simply won't work—you have seen the divorce rates increase and prisons become overcrowded. Both are evidence of families and relationships gone to seed.

I don't give you any guarantee that by doing things my way you'll always be heard; it's been my experience that some people put up barriers that defy any message getting through. You may need to face that reality one day. But I suggest you never give up on a relationship or job without first thoroughly trying the methods in this book. (And perhaps by then I'll have finished my book on *The Wisdom of Giving Up.*)

Anger as a Manipulative Tool

At times, people try to use anger in order to get what they want. Eddie Murphy has a few scenes in "Beverly Hills Cop" in which you can watch him use anger as a social engineering con. Anger as a manipulative trick to get what you want doesn't work for very long. It soon begins to backfire regularly. People who feign anger to get their own way soon wonder how intense the anger has to get before they are heard. Young men and beginning executives realize by the time they get into their thirties that no one reacts to their anger any more; even their kids catch on.

I frequently get requests from men to learn to be assertive as they grow weary of getting angrier and angrier. My goal in this chapter is not to teach you how to use anger to get what you want, but rather to have you learn to express anger in a way that will help you feel better—and still not injure those exposed to your anger.

Insist on the Freedom to Express Your Anger

If someone close to you—boss or co-worker, husband or wife, parent or child—won't accept a new, more honest, more direct behavior from you, tell them calmly, "I want the freedom to express my anger." If they can't accept it, say, "I want to be able to have a relationship with people who are able to accept my anger." Expressing displeasure, frustration and anger is an important freedom for everyone to have. It's one of those freedoms without which you can't be totally you.

Another way to say this, or a way to escalate, goes like this: "Anger is very difficult for people to accept. I want the freedom to express my love and to express my negative feelings, too." If the response you get is still resistant to your expressing anger (even without the word 'you'), let it go for the time being. Then bring it up again at a later date. Sometimes people get used to hearing your requests, and can accept them after a while. It's unwise to expect anyone to hear your request for the first time and say, "Yes." People need the freedom to resist your requests or suggestions.

Expressing anger means saying, "I'm angry—I 'm feeling angry." It does not mean slamming doors or throwing dishes and shouting. An extreme amount or acting out of anger frightens and upsets other people, children especially. The emotional static it causes will interfere with all brain activity, and you'll be the biggest loser because your anger will drive all the other players out of Center Court. You will be playing the game of life alone.

Observe How You Get Angry

What are you like when you get angry? How do you behave? The chances are that you don't accurately know. The next time you lose your temper, I'd like you to observe carefully how you look, what you say, what you do. When my mother got angry she would immediately start some household chore. She'd argue with me, but I had to follow her around while she energetically swept or dusted or washed the dishes. I never saw her eyes while she furiously worked and argued. I sometimes thought she got mad just to get the housework done! My dad would retreat into his study and shut us all out. Mom would get over her anger in an hour or two; when dad was angry, it would take him until the next morning. So I learned the different styles of expressing anger and also how different people get over their anger on different schedules.

...And Observe How Others Get Angry

Some many years ago I worked for a man who insisted on seeing all his direct reports at least once a day. We had a schedule, and I signed up for the 6 p.m. one-on-one—just before going home. The schedule was redone each month, but I always signed up for 6 o'clock. The others thought I was crazy because we worked all over New York City – so I had to come back to the office for my meeting before going home. It was thought lucky to get signed up for a morning meeting. But I wanted the 6 p.m. slot—because I had observed our boss's way with anger.

When he got angry (and he often found something to be angry about), he would hound you all day. He would call around until he tracked you down at a client's, and harangue you over the phone. But I had also observed that by the next morning, whatever had bothered him was gone from his memory and behavior. So I had my 6 o'clock meetings and then went home. By the next morning, he was fine. I never got nagged or bothered. I was free of his anger all day. The others found him offensive but I didn't. A series of people came and then quit, but I went on working for this man for five years and learned a lot from him. He became a mentor of mine and helped me through many career problems. In all those five years, I never had a problem with him because I stuck to that pattern of meeting with him every evening before going home.

For years after, whenever we would meet, he would describe me to others as the best and most perfect employee he ever had. The fact is that I made as many mistakes as those who got fed up and left. I just had figured out how he expressed his anger, and how long it took him to get over it.

Every person and every boss is different. I suggest you get to know what makes them angry, how they show it and how long it takes for them to get over it. Suddenly you'll be able to stay in center court even when someone is angry at you.

Arynne SIMON SAYS:

Unless you know how someone gets angry, you don't really know that person.

Your style of showing anger is an intrinsic part of the real you. Write a description of yourself in anger. Then the next time you get angry, instead of changing your behavior, try to observe more details. Some people raise their voices, while others use non-verbal body language cues to communicate their frustration or fury. Be an observer of your personal style. Method actors are taught to do this so they can replicate it on stage. You may decide that what you do isn't effective, and you may want to refine or alter your style.

Now, with Emotional Fitness training under your belt, you can expect to get angry less frequently as time passes. When it does happen, you'll be more aware of what's going on in the situation and you'll be more able to control the behavior, if not the feeling.

Explain to the people closest to you (but not at work, please) how you get angry. For example, "When I get angry, I slam doors and get busy cleaning dishes." Or "When I get angry I tend to talk a lot and I exaggerate everything." Or "When I get angry, I cry." Or "When I get angry I run for the chocolate candy." Explain, explain, explain—to help others cope and to teach yourself that what you're doing is acting out your anger. And one day you might be aware enough of your own anxious behavior to understand that "when I get frightened I express it in anger."

How you feel at the time you're getting angry is what you say in Box 2: "I'm angry; I'm furious; I wish I were a million miles from here." Tell the truth—describe your feelings in your own words. "I'm upset; I'm out of control; I can't handle this situation." Remember, what goes in Box 3 is what you want, insist, demand be done about the problem in the future. Whatever you do, be sure to talk about the *future*...NOT the *past*. "Next time, let's decide in advance who will give directions." Always 'next time'—a great pair of words.

Arynne SIMON SAYS:

Express life in forward motion and you'll enjoy a sparkling future. If you remind someone what they did wrong in the past—you'll have an argument.

And, hard as it is when you're angry, try to remember that assertively effective language avoids the word 'you.' It's possible to express anger—even extreme anger—without the destructive 'you' accusation. Again, I remind you to say what you want...rather than tell someone else what to do. 'I'm angry' is enough; after all, if you are looking at the person and there-is-no one else in the room, the 'you' word is understood. Getting on a New York subway train doesn't require an extra push with your hands; saying 'you' is like an unneeded push to get onto the train.

And then what...

You'll continue to have those moments or incidents of anger without the ability to apply any of your new behavioral skills. It feels like one step forward and two backward. But be calm and confident. The very fact that you're thinking about how you might have handled the situation differently is a clear win—a chance to learn to do better. So after you've had an angry explosion, I suggest you review the situation and rate your behavior on a scale of 1, the worst, to 10, the best.

Did you remember any of the new skills you learned here? Can you determine where the 'shoulds' are? How about fear? What pushed you out of center court? Did someone press a sensitive button? Can you determine what you really would like in the future? Did you observe any change in your language?

After you experience an explosion of anger, it's a perfect time to review the situation, about how it happened, how it might happen again. You'll be much better able to handle anger in the future when you're able to discuss the way it bubbles up in your life like a volcano with its own unreliable timetable. You can review the material in this book, and slowly learn to coach yourself out of these eruptions.

In Business

People have a plethora of 'shoulds' when it comes to bosses, employees, efficiencies and expectations. It has always been amazing to me that people can work side by side with so few over-reactions. These days when someone explodes, everyone is afraid that it is about to become a media sensation. On the other hand, too many people tend to overlook significant signs of extremely dangerous behavior and are afraid to report it.

But, by and large, the acting out of anger in business is rather limited. Perhaps, if my theory is right, it's because the mind is engaged and one's emotions are put on hold. Yet, too often, holding the emotions in check only lasts until the person gets home. Sad but true; we smile for strangers, and families get the worst of our anger.

Being understanding of the feelings of an employee or frustrated customer is far different than getting emotional about a situation. I would hope that people would bring their human kindness to work, but leave their emotions out of the workplace. This concept may need to be expanded into another book, but I hope you will think about what I am trying to get across. For now, I leave you to make some sense of the difference between feelings and emotions on your own.

There are ways to express the end of your patience when an employee, despite your many verbal nudges, continues to be late to work, to meetings, with turning in deliverables and reports, or in some other way regularly fails to live up to expectations. It's perfectly fine to say, "I'm really angry that I have to talk about lateness and accountability." But first handle your angry emotions by searching for the 'shoulds' behind your anger.

Then design a Three Box statement, with just a single sentence for each, and decide when to say them. If someone comes in late this morning; wait until the afternoon or tomorrow to say, "No one likes meetings. I'm tired of meetings that can't begin on time. In the future, I want everyone on my team in the meeting room five minutes before the announced starting time."

Three sentences—just say them. Keep your communication as laid back as possible and rely on the words only. There is no need to intensify this communication style with a dramatic voice. If you have reminded this person many times in the past, use a different script, such as: "Meetings sometimes seem a waste of time. I have spoken about lateness before. In the future I demand that everyone be ready to start on time, or I will place anyone who is late in the ratings report."

Suppose you have been unfairly dealt with by a store that promised you a refund but has never sent it. Money is due you, and your patience has been exhausted by endless phone calls and letters requesting payment. You are now furious at the way you've been treated. You go to the store to state your case—

Box 1: "It seems there's some money due me, and my letters have explained the history."

Box 2: "I'm angry at the way this has been handled."

Box 3: "I insist on having the check as promised, and I want it now."

If that doesn't get you a "Yes, okay. I'll have the refund issued immediately," continue the conversation by returning to Box 2: "I'm furious this problem is not yet resolved."

And then, Box 3: "I demand my money now."

If you still don't get what you want, back again to Box 2: "I'm really angry and getting even more angry."

Box 3: "I demand the check be written while I wait or I will file an action in small claims court."

Let the person know what the consequences of his neglectful behavior will be. Do not threaten as a way to frighten someone, because it's likely they are used to threats. Express the next step as a logical progression. Stay cool and keep a piece of paper handy to record what is said. And stay in Center Court. If the other person's response to your anger is to overreact in any way, then the best thing for you to do is to leave quickly. As you leave you can remind yourself, "I'm leaving because the situation is out of control. I'm going away to slow it all way down."

Recognize Your Options

As you get to a calmer spot away from the angry scene, you can begin to plot your plan of action. There are always a number of things you can do to solve problems. Keep your brain working and *do not catastrophize.*

In addition to filing in small claims court, you can report the store to the Better Business Bureau. If the person you were speaking with is just an employee, you can track down the owner. If a local television station has a consumer protection program, you can write them a letter and see if they will air a segment on the problem, which would greatly embarrass the store. And so on.

You have a lot of acceptable options that won't make you look foolish and won't get you into trouble with the law or your conscience. Every day for a week you can carry out one of these plans. Slowly but surely, you will set things right.

The Noise Is Outside You

I'm not saying that you'll always get your way. But a lot of experiences are worth living through, even if life gets a bit rough and bumpy. There may come a time when you might understand that the store owner has problems, too; or maybe he's just not smart or capable, and is hanging on to his job by a thread. Perhaps business is bad, or his boss has been leaning on him, or he's just had a string of unhappy customers like you and has been put on warning. You will soon be able, without anger or fear, to get some human perspective on the man and your problem. Some people might call this growing up.

There's a lot happening in everyone's world, and you can manage to deal with whatever comes your way if your mind is working and you stay in Center Court, where there are always many options. By staying rational, you can solve problems and reach agreeable solutions.

When you're angry for any reason, I suggest you say to yourself, "I'm not thinking very clearly now, but if I set my mind to it, I can find a way to solve this problem." Prepare yourself to behave calmly when you call for service of any kind, when you deal with professionals like doctors or dentists, when you make travel plans, deal with credit card companies, visit with in-laws, and take meetings with bosses. Be prepared for some vibration of anger and prepare ahead of time. You'll be ready with a script if anger happens, and you may be delighted to find yourself getting through it. You will not rise to your own rescue with anger as a tool. Your emotional muscles will be primed for life's little glitches.

How Do You Fight?

In order to understand yourself better and, therefore, have greater control over expressing your anger, it's essential to know how you show and express anger. The way you handle anger will reflect your personality as much as your walk or your style of handwriting or your favorite sleeping position. When you are able to describe your method of arguing, fighting, manipulating and controlling others, you will finally be able to say you know yourself.

When angry, my style is to use voice volume and a plethora of words. My voice gets gradually louder as I get angrier. My husband, on the other hand, starts with silence and a deep, thoughtful frown, and suddenly, zoom: with no advanced warning he gets his voice and it's strong enough to be shocking.

There are people who shrug their shoulders, say "That's ridiculous," and stomp out of the room to sulk. Others use obscenities, threats, or accusations. Sarcasm and put downs are angry aggressive humor. Silent brooding is another method, and it may be the most insidious form of anger. Some people smile while expressing angry words and the double signal of that style delivers a double whammy. You don't know your boss until you know what makes him/her angry, how he/she shows anger, and how long the anger lasts.

I encourage you to know how you get angry and be courageous about letting others who are important to you know your style. Then people who are close to you can know you more precisely and have success in dealing with you. The best part of this can be that you will be left alone to get over your anger in your own way.

Say You're Sorry

To be human is to be imperfect, and that means even offending people you deeply care about. Especially at moments of extreme upset, you will hurt another. But there's no need to feel an excessive amount of guilt or shame. You can be sorry about it, and there is a time and place to express that.

There's not a parent or significant other who hasn't wished at some time or other that their loved ones would just disappear. Those moods and mental images are part of human reality. The expression of that feeling as an angry attack is definitely something to be sorry for, because at that moment you *intended* to hurt someone else, and you did. If you accidentally bump into someone on the street, you graciously apologize. And if you hurt someone's feelings in a moment of anger, you can afterward tell them you're sorry for having hurt them.

There are fun ways to do this, and I urge you to be creative. In his poignant book *Love Story*, author Erich Segal observes, "Love means never having to say you're sorry." So, okay, let's leave 'sorry' out of your vocabulary. Recently I said something to my husband too quickly, and it sounded like an angry comment very much overstated. So I said to him (appropriately, since he is a film writer as well as an author), "I don't like the way that scene was written; I'd like to write it differently. Let's play it again."

This is a time for you to get creative with your language so that your relationships will stay in Center Court right through your anger, your fear and your inappropriate use of aggressive language rather than emotionally fit assertive communication.

ARYNNE **SIMON SAYS:**

A person is emotionally fit in proportion to the comfort with which he/she takes 'no' for an answer.

Envoi

Whether in business, in life, and maybe even on the playing field, the true competitor is never the one whose team name is up on a banner or scoreboard.

Somehow I was lucky—or maybe just blind—but I have always tried to do my very best without trying to pinpoint who my competitor really was. I just, as they say, did my own thing. The master painter Renoir, when asked to advise a young artist, suggested that he not look at the work of other painters, but rather study nature and study the Masters. Perhaps Renoir's advice is wise for all of us to follow as we seek to survive the many problems that life dishes out.

During my life I have had to conquer only one opponent, and that adversary is me. By now, I believe the only real competitor any of us has is ourselves. The negative messages delivered to me by internal voices learned along the way have too often diminished my levels of determination and confused my goals. Fighting one's own inner voices takes true bravery.

In business, I suggest you keep clearly in mind the advice of Renoir and ignore everything except where you are going and what you hope to accomplish. But do not ignore people along the way. In

Buddhist terms: "Live every day as though you will live forever, while at the same time living every day as if it's the last day of your life." When you can put these together, you will have the deepest sort of emotional fitness.

I think you will agree that my Emotional Fitness method will not only redirect your anger and fear, but will increase your courage to be as close to living at 100 percent as a person can be. And in my opinion, therein lies true freedom.

Many people believe that freedom comes with money or success. Not true. Freedom is hard won. Money only takes care of money problems. Money is an important chunk of life, and worth working for, but emotional and relationship problems still exist among the super rich.

It's emotional freedom—not money—that is the infrastructure of all other freedoms. Lessons like the ones in this book give you the kind of emotional freedom that is the foundation of contentment. I want the lessons you have learned from this book to be your private gold mine for emotional wealth.

Afterword

Those who take my courses and hear my speeches have heard me ask at the conclusion, "What one thing have you learned today that will make a difference in your life tomorrow?" And from each participant I hear a different response. One might say that life is sure to be improved when one realizes the significant difference between instructions and suggestions. Another believes that the definition of what makes a 'good' day — knowing what you want and having the courage to say it out loud — is surely the secret to a better life.

Someone else praises the module that encourages knowing what you want. Then maybe a man in the back who always came in late after the breaks says that life with his family is sure to be better now that he understands what quality listening is all about. He proves to me that he has learned the lesson well because he then leads the group into a perceptive discussion by asking questions. As you can well imagine, these varied responses warm my heart.

So, after hearing all the positive responses and the applause which I admit enjoying, I encourage the group to give me a second chance at convincing them if something I've said seems to annoy their brain. I want to try explaining my ideas differently if any resistance is getting in the way of someone learning.

For example, I know that over the years students have taken issue with one of my statements about anger — that it is like teenage acne and can for the most part be outgrown. The psychological commu-

185

nity has worked hard and long to convince people that showing anger is a good thing. Why, oh why, would I want someone to hide their anger and submerge it again? That seems like taking a giant step backwards. So I patiently explain to those who might have misinterpreted what I meant that feeling anger and expressing it openly in an assertive way is far different than breaking out with the kind of destructive anger that damages both the giver and the getter, leaving victims with bruising, scars and sad memories, and the desire to escape.

If you have points that you disagreed with, I'd like to suggest that you go back over that part of the book again; perhaps if you read it slowly and carefully the second time, you may pick up something that will give me a second chance to convince you. I'd appreciate that.

Since you are a reader and not part of one of my theatre or classroom audiences, you are not able to verbally resist my ideas on the spot and engage me in discussion. But I am therefore also put at a disadvantage because I don't have the opportunity to describe what I mean in another way and correct your perception of what I have put forward. So I have a limited chance to convince you. But I do encourage you to write me via email (arynne@simon1.com) or via snail mail care of my publisher, SelectBooks, in New York. But first I encourage you to reread any passage that contains a message you would like to take issue with.

Maybe you will still resist. Resistance is the sign of an intelligent mind at work. I both understand your resistance and admire it. Very dull people are often too easily convinced and, therefore, less resistant. People with spirit and fast minds demand to hold on to their own perceptions and ideas, even the ones that don't seem to be working.

In a very real sense, by offering you this book I'm expecting you to revolutionize your thinking and feelings. Evolutionary change comes naturally, but happens over time. There is nothing so revolutionary in my ideas that you might not have learned on your own during the years ahead, but it's my intent to help you acquire new behaviors on a much faster timetable.

Yes, you would have had your own moments of revelation and transformation without me. Typically, growth and change are the result of the pain you experience. I am sure you would have realized that your feelings had evolved and changed; life often gets better as a result of experience. However, better behaviors need to be designed and tested. Perhaps you, as I have done, can design some for yourself—and after testing them you can teach them to others. Or perhaps you can accept these emotional fitness skills that are based on my pain, frustration and experience, and have been tested. Save yourself years of pain, and instead learn to play piano or enroll in art school or pick up a career you left on the shelf some years ago. There's more to life than learning how to live it.

Rapid transformations add excitement and energy to existence while the subtle changes often go unnoticed. I hope you will enjoy experiencing all changes and growth. I also hope you will reach for this book to read again and again — for, like a diet, you could slip back into some old patterns of thinking and behavior without me near to nag you.

But no matter whether you are convinced or not, things will never be quite the same for you again. By reading this book, you have developed a whole new set of listening skills and new perceptions — and a set of new and better expectations. Even though you will continue to be critical of the behavior of others, I hope you will be more accepting of people despite their inevitable imperfections. And that you will live life in forward motion and protect everyone from the pain of going backwards. You have learned to stop asking 'why' and have learned to ask the type of questions that begin with 'if.'

One of the most quoted lines of Will Rogers, who was outspokenly critical of politicians, institutions, and causes, was that he never met a man he didn't like. My husband finally decided that Rogers probably meant he had never met anyone he couldn't learn something from. But I interpret Rogers' famous line rather differently; I believe it was a way he expressed his acceptance of an individual, even while he was critical of organized groups. If I'm right, then I can say that I'm a lot like Will Rogers ... because I've never met a person I didn't like.

At my in-person sessions, someone usually asks me which one of my own lessons I consider most important. I have a fleeting thought that I have taught these people too well and that the questions are getting harder and harder to answer.

But, yes, I have an answer to that question. In my view, it's vitally important to remember that anxiety is the result of the combination of Anger *and* Fear. It's the fear part of this equation that most people have trouble admitting. Call it what you will—dread, feeling trapped, whatever—but I encourage you to courageously search for it until you find that emotional chemical of Fear in each situation that causes all explosions. If you can learn to express it to another person, you will help build a stronger relationship and de-escalate your feeling of fear. If you can remember only one part of all you've learned, this is what I would choose for you.

So stay in Center Court, stay emotionally fit, and stay in touch. When you feel like another boost, visit my Web site at www.arynne.com, and read some of the "Arynne SIMON SAYS" entries—short articles that will give you a quick pick-me-up from whatever is troubling you. And get ready for the next book I have already begun to write.

You can reach Arynne Simon by writing to:

Wilarvi Communications, Inc.
Box 2048
Rancho Santa Fe, CA 92067

If you would like to order a set of Arynne's Assertive Behavior tape cassette program, or any of her other tapes, or if you would like to read other essays by Dr. Simon, visit: www.arynne.com